Gari Stein's

The More We Get Together

Nurturing Relationships Through Music, Play, Books and Art

publishing house of RoseyRaeNate productions

Ann Arbor, Michigan

www.little-folks-music.com

The author has made every effort to trace ownership of copyrighted materials and to secure permission from copyright holders. If there is any question regarding ownership, any necessary corrections will be made in future publications.

littefolksters™ is a registered trademark of Gari Stein

Library of Congress Cataloging-in-Publication Data

Stein, Gari R.
   The more we get together : nurturing relationships through music, play, books, and art / by Gari R. Stein.
        p. cm.
   Includes bibliographical references.
   ISBN 978-0-935356-00-4
   1. Play. 2. Child development. 3. Arts and children. I. Title.
   HQ782.S73 2008
   790.1'91--dc22
                          2008039633

Manufactured in the United States of America

To everyone near and far, large and small, who helped feed this Journey.
I am blessed to have you in my life.

"The Very Thought of You…"
To Ira, my partner, a constant source of strength, always cheering me on.
To my children, Jon and Maggie, and to their spouses, Leslie and Matt.
They fill me with memories of childhood, theirs and mine.
To Kailey, Ella and Nathan, my precious grandchildren, who take me to the most beautiful of all places
and put up with my endless singing of songs marking every possible occasion.

In loving memory of my Mother Ruth, Sister Margie and Aunt Dorothy,
who sang with me all the days of their lives.

When I was just a little girl, I asked my mother, what will I be?
Will I be pretty, will I be rich? Here's what she said to me:
"Que sera, sera. Whatever will be, will be, will be.
The future's not ours to see. Que sera, sera."
—Ray Evans

To my Guardian Angels, Ruth and Sol Stein, and Kathleen and Manny Lax.

To my brother Bob and dearest friends, Audrey, Becky and Josh, who give me courage.

To my cousin Susan, who made it possible for me to become an independent publisher.

To Mrs. Keppel, my music teacher at Hampton Elementary in Detroit, Michigan, for early inspiration.
Her passion and tears fostered my love of traditional music. And to Anne Zirulnik, whose invitation to
join the Dance Club at Mumford High School was a turning point in my life.

To the families at Music for Little Folks—all the families I have worked with and all of those that I hope
to meet in the coming years. I am eternally grateful for the opportunity to touch so many lives.
Without you, for me, there would be no music.

In blessed memory of my students Margaret, Simon, Sam and Juliana,
whose sweet songs touched so many during their short time on earth.

This fun and educational resource is chockfull of the benefits of music-making, personal experiences, easy to understand research, parenting tips, family stories, and lots of activities for tots to eights, with a special section devoted to infants. The "Sing With Me" CD series is filled with all aspects of music-making activities to bring the program home or into any venue that serves the needs of families.

Mention this coupon for a 10 percent discount off any order from my website: http://www.little-folks-music.com.

CONTENTS

FROM THE AUTHOR

Welcome to

The More We Get Together

My teaching career began at age twelve in my basement in Detroit, Michigan, with dance classes for the neighborhood children. After five decades I am still at it holding weekly music and movement classes in my studio. My family is my life, and my work is my life's passion. My three young grandchildren seem to put up with my continual use of song to mark every possible occasion.

Music For Little Folks was born in 1993. It has been a privilege to expose hundreds of children and their families to a rich musical environment. I have had the honor to partner with the Ann Arbor Symphony to create a program especially for these precious little ones. Staff development and family concerts have increased in Michigan and throughout the Midwest. I look forward to taking *The More We Get Together* around the entire country with my Sing With Your Baby-Juice and Crackers Tour.

My hope is that this book will bring you lots of ideas and information about nurturing these most essential relationships. Please take time to enjoy the photos that quietly demonstrate how music and the related arts can fill your homes and classrooms with joy and peace. When you share these simple activities with young children you are giving them gifts that will last a lifetime. When all else fails, read a book, play with abandon, draw and paint, be in nature, sing a song and dance along. It really works!

Cari Stein

PREFACE

Mommy, Daddy, Granny, Nanny, Teachers, Librarians Too…Sing and Play, Read and Draw…It's Fun and Good for You!

Several years ago, I set out on this journey of writing, with the value of music in a young child's life my original focus. My research, however, took me in many compelling directions, far beyond the music.

The role of play and its contribution to the healthy development of the whole child came up recurrently, and how literature and the creative arts impact the growth of young children soon became central to my quest. As an educator, I had witnessed firsthand from the little ones that these are not isolated components, but an integral part of their everyday routine.

Music, play, literature, dance and art affect one's physical, emotional, social and spiritual growth; all are intertwined in the child's world. The strength of their impact on the primary relationships young children form was brought home to me through my life's work in the studio, in the classroom and on the concert stage. Music, then, remains the focus here, but play spills over throughout, culminating in later sections devoted to literature, creative movement and art.

And music itself is never just music: it's a way to nurture relationships as a song, story, poem, or waltz creates a precious moment in time to be shared together.

It is only by introducing the young to great literature, drama and music, and to the excitement of great science that we open to them the possibilities that lie within the human spirit—enable them to see visions and dream dreams.
—Eric Anderson

ACKNOWLEDGMENTS

Without the following folks, to whom I am eternally grateful, my book would have remained in a box rather than finding a place in the lives of young children and their families.

Maria Coolican, mother of Liam and Mary Katharine, made my navigation of the confusing world of cyberspace possible.

Mary Bisbee-Beek's kindness and generosity allowed this book to leave the computer.

Carol Sickman-Garner, mother of Lily and Robin, with attention to every detail, combined her professional talent with her maternal instincts to edit this book.

Erin Howarth of Wilderness Books guided me from concept to completion, layout design and photos, with expertise and enthusiasm.

Kate Uleman, mother of Sahara, designed the cover with patience and grace.

I thank the gracious staffs at the Ann Arbor District Library, the Ypsilanti District Library and the Ann Arbor Symphony, and Denise Glesser of Progressive Book Marketing, who give me a stage.

Mike Tanner of World Class Tapes for his kindness and skills in graphic design and to Earl, Kevin and Matt for their amazing customer service.

Sweet Sue Gills, of WCT, has gone far beyond her professional role in coordinating all aspects of producing my music and educational materials.

I am also grateful to Randall Beek, Julie Benben, Patrick Borelli, Max Fabick, Chin Kim of Focus Photo, Cassie Murdoch and Ken Wachsberger.

OVERTURE

And So It Begins…My First Music Lesson

Ah-ah, ah-ah baby,
Mama is a lady
Daddy is a gentleman
And you're the little baby
—Traditional lullaby

Take a moment. Close your eyes and try to remember your first childhood memory of being sung to.

Held close and rocked in my mother's arms: "Ah-Ah Baby" was my first introduction to music. This special bedtime ritual grew to become an integral part of my childhood, the rocking replaced by a hand gently tapping my back, lulling me to sleep. It became a tradition that I have passed down to my children and now my grandchildren in helping them get ready for sleep. I just need to say "Ah-ah" to the newest little one, and down she goes on her tummy, arms stretched over her head for me to pat her back as I recite the rhyme. At twenty months, she repeats it while she pats her dollies.

I spent my formative years as the lone chorus girl in the living room, on my make-believe stage. Little did I know that my song-and-dance routines, along with camp musicals, would create the foundation of my subsequent life's work.

Being a young mom in the late 1960s, I hadn't been formally educated about music and movement. Yet somehow, I knew to play Tchaikovsky's *Nutcracker Suite* for my little ones at bedtime. It helped give them an early appreciation of good

music that they could pass along to their children. Just from driving to and from Grandma's house, my two-year-old granddaughter requested Mozart on road trips and knew the difference if I played Handel. The four-year-old liked singing her ABCs but also loved humming the melodies from Handel's *Water Music,* note for note. When I sing with my grandson, it's often via the Web cam, and just recently I saw him, at twenty-six months, drumming with a very steady beat. A professional drummer saw the video and thought he kept a better beat than many adults he knows, and he wasn't kidding. One heart-warming grandma memory is of my granddaughter at age three, walking through the woods, stopped in her tracks to belt out "Somewhere over the Rainbow" with such feeling it would have made Judy Garland proud.

When I was a young teacher working in the classroom, music and movement were always an integral part of my curriculum. I realized early on the value of early musical experiences, not just in the classroom, as an activity to fill time, but as a tool that carries over into the everyday world of the young child.

In the early 1990s, approaching my sixth

decade, I ventured out on my own and began an educational and personal journey into the power of music and movement in early childhood. Fortunate to have studied with many experts, I quickly realized that my early instincts were right on: music is essential to the young child and basic to human survival. Research supports this conclusion, and my hands-on experience uncovers its true value.

I saw a need not being met and extended my work throughout the Midwest to include staff development and family programming. The response from attendees affirmed that I was onto something. Educators and families were yearning for developmentally appropriate activities for their little ones. Requests for my services soon followed from social service agencies and libraries.

Most commercially produced children's music is often too loud, too fast, too busy and not really geared toward the youngest of us. I went on to create the "Sing With Me" music series for tots to eights, with a consistent emphasis on parenting, partner activities and hard-to-find ideas specifically for infants to threes.

I came to realize that a lot more than music happens at music time. Brains are nourished, growth and development are impacted, and a profound interaction takes place between the little ones and the grown-ups who love them. Everyone, young and old, has a great time. The music is fun, and it feels good. And now the research bears out just how grand music really is—for the mind, body and soul. When all else fails, sing a song and dance along. It really works! No musical talent or expense required.

The More We Get Together brings together everything I know about music, dance, literature, drama and art, children, families and parenting, while providing numerous hands-on activities, encouragement and support. It's all here: a resource every parent, caregiver and teacher will want to use every day.

Connecting with folks, building relationships and bringing families and educators simple tools to help make life a little easier is immensely gratifying. I am happy, now, to share my dream with all of you.

Grandma Love

For me, one of life's greatest pleasures is singing and dancing with my grandchildren. I hope that grandparents reading this guide will be reminded of the special traditions they enjoyed as children that can now be shared with their precious little ones, perhaps finding some new ways to connect through music.

To sidestep the subject for a moment, I would like to share an important parenting lesson I learned when I became a grandparent. Having had so many years of experience, I felt it was okay to offer suggestions to my children about how to raise and care for little ones. One of my grown children brought me back to reality, and fast. After I volunteered one suggestion too many, I was lovingly told that my advice made my children question their parenting skills. That was all I had to hear.

I still slip now and then, but I make a conscious effort to keep my opinions to myself. If you want to have a good relationship with your children and their spouses or partners, think about what I try to do now. Put on your listening ears, and give your lips a zip-zip-zip. Enjoy your grandchildren. Give them lots and lots of grandma/grandpa love and leave the child rearing to their parents—the good, the bad and the ugly. After all, it's all about the relationships.

The More We Get Together is presented in two parts. The first focuses on exciting research in the field, presented in clear terms and designed to guide you to many additional resources. Read about the power of music in families' lives; the connections among music, language and literacy, the importance of play, listening and hearing; and the special world of infants.

The second focuses on ideas and activities and guides you to even more resources. Find ideas for activities to share at home or in a group, with infants and toddlers, preschool-age children and older children. This section includes a potpourri of partner, listening and transitional activities; seasonal celebrations; play parties and singing games; and a guide to books, art, lullabies and authentic children's musicians from all over the country.

The songs and chants cited throughout *The More We Get Together* can be heard on the "Sing With Me" series of CDs, which include words, motions and specific directions. A DVD is also available that gives you lots of ideas for structuring a class or doing activities at home.

Sharing the Love with Picture Books

- *Grandma's Beach,* by Rosalind Beardshaw
- *Grandfather Twilight,* by Barbara Berger
- *The Puddleman,* by Raymond Briggs
- *Wilfrid Gordon McDonald Partridge,* by Mem Fox
- *Balloons for Grandpa* and *Little Bear's Grandpa,* by Nigel Grey
- *And the Good Brown Earth,* by Kathy Henderson
- *Mr. George Baker,* by Amy Hest
- *The Giant Hug,* by Sandra Horning
- *The Beeman,* by Laurie Krebs
- *My Little Grandmother Often Forgets,* by Reeve Lindbergh
- *It's Too Soon!* by Nigel McMulllen
- *What Grandmas/Grandpas do Best,* by Laura Numeroff
- *Vera's Baby Sister,* by Vera Rosenberry

Part 1
THE RESEARCH
Much More Than Just the Facts

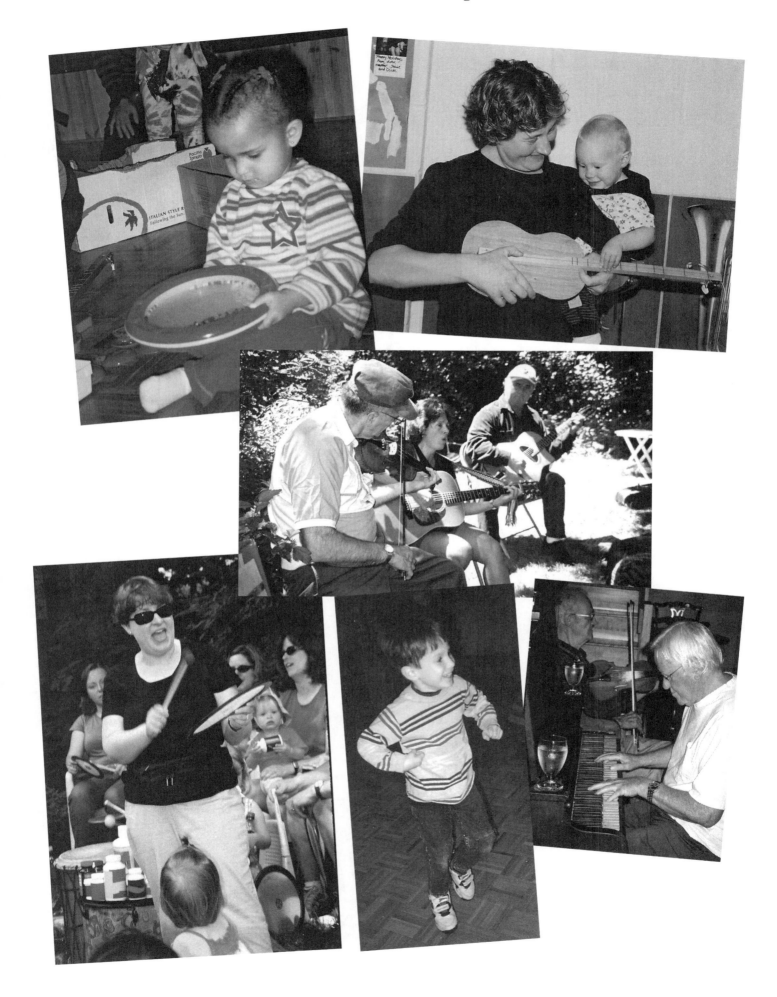

THE POWER OF MUSIC

Music is vitamin M. Music is a chocolate chip in the cookie of life.
—**Paul Lehman,** *Why Study Music in School?*

How can I keep from singing?
—**Robert Lowry (1860)**

Woody Guthrie speaks about the power of voices together, and Pete Seeger writes songs that people can sing together. The music of these two masters is always a staple in any community sing I have attended. East Lansing, Michigan, has hosted the Annual Mid-Winter Singing Festival for the past six years. This event started with the vision of one woman—a woman who loves to sing and believed the community would too. Voices, large and small, young and old, harmonious and off-key, join together in song, each contributing to a spirit so powerful that it almost becomes a religious experience. The festival begins and ends with the song "How Can I Keep from Singing?" (1860). Hearing this song sung by so many is a profound experience all by itself.[1]

Everything about good music is positive, with the power to affect our lives forever. In our hurry-up dot-com world, musical experiences provide a sense of community and belonging. A simple song, readily available, can help slow things down.

Music is also a powerful way for children to connect to their roots. A spiritual, lullaby or folk song can introduce a baby to her or his heritage in a way that goes beyond words or pictures. Connecting to their roots makes children feel safe and secure.

The richness of traditional folk music, using old tunes in new ways: such simple tools allow families to bond with each other. A parent might reconnect with childhood memories of sitting with a grandparent in the kitchen or on the front porch, singing songs and sharing hugs, laughter and special moments. Relationships are formed that last a lifetime.

"[In] a six-month study of 60 recent stroke victims, researchers in Finland found that exposure to music for at least one hour a day improved verbal memory. Brain exposure to music led to a boost in concentration tasks. The study suggests that music-listening could be used as a leisure activity that might provide comfort and help cognitive recovery."
—Teppo Sarkamo, University of Helsinki Department of Psychology and the Helinski Brain Research Center

---

[1] The melody and lyrics can be accessed at http://www.cyberhymnal.org/htm/h/c/hcaikeep.htm.

"Hi-Ho, the Derry-O": Music Does Not Stand Alone

Music washes away from the soul the dust of everyday life.
—Berthold Auerbach (1812–1882)

As my musical journey evolved, it became increasingly clear that much more than just music was happening. Music becomes a vehicle for language exploration; movement incorporates action words and spatial relationships; drawings lead to letters and words. Drama and storytelling bring together all of the arts for activities in the home and can easily form the basis of an entire yearlong curriculum in the classroom.

Children are born musicians, dancers, artists and storytellers, and the opportunities for healthy development are endless. We just have to provide the canvas, the paper, the paints, the materials and the welcoming environment, setting the stage for creativity, learning and fun. Can't we try to deemphasize the ABCs and reemphasize what comes naturally to young children? Not only will the children's environment brighten, but adults will find that stress decreases and productivity and efficiency increase. It really is so simple.

And just in case you can't fathom giving up the ABCs, let me assure you that throughout all this play and fun, learning does happen. It happened for me, it happened for you, and it will happen for all of our children if we give them the time to experience their childhood.

Whistle a Happy Tune

All the sounds of the earth are like music.
—Oscar Hammerstein, "Oh, What a Beautiful Morning"

As our children's first teachers, we have perhaps the most important job there is. Children learn about the world from us, about love and trust. Childhood lays the foundation for who we become as adults; it is the wellspring of lifelong memories. In this hurry-up world, however, there seems to be less and less family time.

In our sophisticated technological lives, young children still need what they have always needed: to feel safe and loved; to be hugged, rocked, read and sung to. They need time to explore, ride bikes, swing on swings, make art, solve problems. They need to be listened to; they need time to just be. Write down their stories, tape-record their songs. Spend time outdoors, on the floor, building with blocks, sharing books. Make space for art, for water and sand play. Take nature walks—splash together in puddles and sit together in silence. Share a song, bake a cake from scratch, dance with abandon, whistle

---

Musical activities in early childhood can

- Instantly transform a cranky mood into a mood of joy and harmony
- Provide a safe avenue for self-expression
- Support individual learning styles, independence and creativity
- Help children adjust to being part of a group
- Model parenting skills and strengthen the adult-child bond
- Relieve stress for adult staff, heightening their efficiency and productivity
- Teach patterning, rhythm, sequencing, coordination
- Sharpen listening skills

Studies suggest that music and movement

- Nourish the brain while affecting all areas of development
- Strengthen listening, motor skills, language, problem solving, spatial-temporal performance and literacy
- Help develop critical-thinking skills
- Create space for emotional well-being
- Provide opportunities to practice social skills
- Support phonemic awareness
- Instill acts of kindness and cooperation
- Calm and focus the mind
- Encourage interaction in non-threatening ways

a happy tune, create an environment that says yes more often than no.

If we want a peaceful world, we need to be peaceful. Music can bring this quality of life to all of us. If you can talk, you can sing; if you can move, you can dance. Music is for everyone, not just the little ones. When we give children opportunities to experience the joy of making music, we give them a gift that will last a lifetime. Donna Brink Fox, of the Eastman School of Music, tells us, "We know it's true that music in early childhood can make a difference in children's lives. But it's also important to understand that early music experience can affect people for years to come."

When I first began researching the power of music in our lives, I was extremely blessed to study with many early childhood music experts. One of my most treasured experiences was spending time studying with Edwin Gordon, who created "music learning theory," and Cynthia Crump Taggart, who helped develop it. From them and several of their colleagues, I learned about audiation, silence, resting tones, melodies, child-centered approaches and much more. Over the years I have gathered many techniques, incorporating them into my repertoire, but nothing has

impacted me professionally as much as this approach to music and movement.

Cynthia Crump Taggart tells us that "research from the last 30 years has shown us that the quality of the music environment surrounding children affects their lifelong potential to interact with music in a meaningful way." The National Association for the Education of Young Children (NAEYC), she reminds us, stresses that children are not "little adults" and that they therefore learn in different ways.

Taggart offers a rich array of suggestions. While much of her content is directed toward teachers in an educational setting, much is also relevant to parents, with activities and ideas that can be adapted to daily family routines and home life. Again, making music becomes a means of parenting.

Here, I want to share some of Taggart's key points that really speak to my philosophy of working with young children and their families:

- Children "play" with language by engaging in language babble. Taggart recommends singing for children, not with them, so they can hear music.

- It is in a young child's best interest that there are no expectations of correctness. They may or may not be developmentally ready to make music "correctly" by first or second grade.

Taggart points out that "some children choose to simply sit and watch what is happening in the music class." I find this to be one of the hardest aspects of parenting for adults. If they don't see any visible, immediate interaction, they may find it hard to believe that their child is participating. Later, however, at home, they often see that their child has absorbed more than they could have ever imagined.

This dynamic often plays into my biggest struggle as an educator, and it's also a common source of frustration for my colleagues who work with families. My message is, "Leave your expectations at the door. Let your child explore the materials in the manner he or she chooses." C. Hornbach is clear about the importance of "letting go" with our children:

- To meet young children's educational needs, we must let go of our expectations that every child be "on task" all of the time. Instead, we need to give them the time and space to explore and construct their own musical meanings and knowledge.

- Eliciting responses from children requires that we include silent moments, for it is in these silent moments that children respond. Taggart goes even further:

- Young children benefit from repetition: revisiting music and activities experienced earlier facilitates and solidifies learning. (When I conduct staff development, I emphasize the three Rs: repeat, repeat, repeat.)

- Children need a balance of songs with and without text. Songs without text give children the opportunity to focus on the musical elements without being distracted and facilitate their creation of spontaneous songs.

Musical activities often include an emphasis on keeping the beat, as it has been suggested that awareness of rhythm helps with reading. Taggart points out that all early childhood music environments should include movement, but she goes on to stress that "first children need to move fluidly and continuously through space... freely, without emphasis on beat....We should also have children explore creative movement and help them become aware of the movements of their bodies before and as we focus on beat."

Dee Joy Coulter concurs, describing "songs, movement and musical games of childhood as brilliant neurological exercises that introduce children to speech patterns, sensory motor skills and vital movement strategies." "Music activities combining rhythmic movement with speech and song," she tells us, "benefit children by providing opportunities to develop the mind further."

Experts on education consistently view children's early musical experiences as a core component of development. Lorna Heyge views music as a "preclinical dose of treatment utilizing speech, motor development and sensory integration." Music, according to Heyge:

- Optimizes brain development
- Enhances multiple intelligences
- Facilitates genuine bonding
- Builds social/emotional skills
- Promotes attention to tasks and inner speech
- Encourages impulse control and motor development
- Communicates creativity and joy

The Instrumental Question…To Play or Not to Play?

One of the most common questions I am asked by parents is when they should start giving their children private instrument lessons. I went to the best source I know to help answer this question. The Early Childhood Music and Movement Association (ECMMA) was organized in 1986. Rick Townsend, its managing director, tells me, "the organization was originally organized in 1986 for uniting early childhood music teachers…and broadened its base in 1996 to include all who invest their lives in children through music and movement."

ECMMA's advisory board is a "who's-who" of experts in the field of early childhood music and development, all invested in the well-being of young children and their families. ECMMA's shared purpose is stated as follows:

- To be an advocate for joyful music and movement and experiences vital to the development of the whole child.

- To further the advancement and development of music and movement education for young children.

- To serve the needs and encourage ongoing professional development of educators in music and other areas of early childhood education.

- To support family structure by encouraging positive interaction between parents and children through the sharing of music.[2]

In addition to its stellar board, ECMMA's general membership, from across the country and around the world, consists of dedicated music teachers of the highest quality. I have had the opportunity to study with some of these fine educators, and I have met others via the group's extraordinary listserv.

Recently, the topic of when to begin instrument lessons came up. I want to share some of these teachers' responses:

Julie Goodro, Murray, Utah

Age? It depends on the child, parent and teacher. And it isn't necessary to start with a half-hour lesson. Five-minute lessons are very valuable for very young children. Very small steps can be taken profitably with 2 and 3 years olds (and older) who show an interest. That doesn't mean they are being required to have a "sit still, be quiet, listen to me," lesson. Doctor Suzuki was very playful with children.

A lesson can be daily for only a few minutes to create a routine and prepare the ground. I have heard teachers who don't believe there is any value to starting so young. They say, "wait until they can read" so they can begin with notation. And I have taught that way myself. But in learning about the brain, the eyes and ears need separate training. If reading is the focus, the ears learn less. (How many of our students don't really listen to themselves if they learned notation first?) If the ear is the focus the eyes must learn their part in a different time. Both need to be taught, but not the same way.

There are several programs that gradually bring in the instrument along with whole body movement for a deeper understanding of rhythm and pitch, phrase etc. I'm all for GRADUALLY bringing in the discipline of a sit-down lesson, watching the child and stopping BEFORE they run out of attention. Kids also learn a lot from being in the same room as someone else [who] is having a lesson, hence the whole value of "teaching" the parent or being present for a sibling's or any other child's lesson, long before the child

2 See ECMMA's Web site at http://www.ecmma.org.

is required to "perform" at their own lesson.

Though cost may be prohibitive, it would be great if children could attend any wonderful group music class and have another music experience focused a little more on the instrument. Most of us can't afford such a luxury, but we can fill our homes with music and look for child friendly community music experiences. The parent is generally the key here. Some of these programs are a combination of group and instrument lessons. Some teachers bring in more instruments than others in whatever program they are teaching. You're lucky if you can find one (or be the teacher of one). There are many options for many different situations of parents and children. Let's just keep the music coming.

Mary Ellen Moravec-Newsom, Bolingbrook, Illinois (m.e.newsom@comcast.net)

When children have listened for a year and a half or more to the recordings and practicing of older siblings, they are ready to play the tunes for themselves at the piano or on the violin. Others are not ready at this point. Wait. They will be ready soon. I utilize whatever method/material is "out there" so that the child's needs and learning style can be met. When I began teaching, we had barely heard of the Suzuki method. I continually investigate new materials and new methods—anything and everything on the market—to best match materials to students.

Generally speaking, girls are ready for lessons at the age of 2 and definitely by the age of 3. I don't accept boys until about age 4½ to 5 for private lessons on any instrument—regardless of how badly the parent wants lessons for them. Parents may feel their children have special musical aptitude when they "move with the music" that is being played

or "sing along" when music is playing. As teachers we know that most children do these things and that we would worry about them if they *didn't* move with the music or sing at the top of their lungs at the top of the backyard slide.

Little kids can learn *huge* things musically long before they can read notes. Note reading can very easily come later and for many kids, it's only possible much later. I do teach children to read music. However, I do it *very* gradually and I don't push it when the brain seems to be preoccupied with body growth or just isn't ready to accept more input. Some kids learn to read music just by having the music in front of them when they play. They learn that "allegro" means fast because that's how they play the song called "Allegro."

Many very young children have a huge amount of natural talent. Younger siblings of children studying music, particularly, have a great deal of listening experience and have already developed quite an "ear." Parents can provide music listening experiences in the home. Those parents who play can and should play for their children to hear and—most importantly—see and realize that Mom/Dad place *value* on music/playing an instrument/singing. We teach by example.

Christa Sigman, Albany, Ohio (http://www.kindermusik.com)

I personally prefer my piano students to have a concept of alphabet and reading left to right before I start them. I do require all my beginners, if they are children, regardless of age, to start with no more than 15-minute lessons. Only about 5–10 of that is actually on the bench. I tend to carry my movement and whole body ideas into my private teaching.

The Mother and Child Reunion

In October of 2007, a symposium was held at the University of Michigan on the evolutionary value of art and why humans spend so much time at it. Ellen Dissanayake, an independent scholar affiliated with the University of Washington, has an idea about how art got its start from the intimate interplay between mother and child. The explanation may be a bit technical, but I whooped out a big "wow" when I read it, and I feel it's worth sharing, as it further affirms how parent-child interaction contributes to the healthy development of our children. In this scenario, it's directly related to the arts.

Dissanayake compares the rituals that bond mother and child to the techniques and construction that "are at the heart of our art." She identifies universal traits that define the mother-infant bond: "They are visual, gestural and vocal cues that arise spontaneously and unconsciously between mothers and infants, but they nevertheless abide by a formalized code: the calls and responses, the swooping bell tones of motherese, the widening of the eyes, the exaggerated smile, the repetitions and variations, the laughter of the baby met by the mother's emphatic refrain."

To Dissanayake, these bonding rituals look a lot like art: "These signals between mother and infant are aesthetic operations, and aesthetic operations are what artists do—using the tools that mothers everywhere have used for hundreds of generations."

Definitely sweet food for thought.

Every Child Is Special

Music's power also extends to those children who might seem challenging to reach—and it gives these children the ability to "reach" back. When I get a call asking if I take children with special needs in my classes, I am reminded of a simple philosophy: every child is special, and every child has a special need. I find that music speaks to all children, regardless of where they are developmentally.

Recently, as my work on this book was coming to an end, I read an email request for materials for a "special ed." assembly. It was then I came across Deborah Stuart, an educator in New Hampshire and Florida (Debstuart11@msn.com) whose work takes her around the country and abroad, conducting trainings that focus on the role of the arts in learning. Her specialty is music in early education, particularly as it relates to children and young people who have different learning needs and/or abilities. Her message is so eloquently written that I want to share it.

"The most important thing," Stuart writes, "is to keep your approach age appropriate. In other words, you can use very 'young' songs but you have to do them in a humorous way—think of if somebody told you that you were going to sing 'Wheels on the Bus' with typical teenagers and think what you would do with that—you'd ham it up, put in more clever words, etc. This will work well with an amazing number of songs we think of as ones for little ones."

Stuart goes on to say that "kids with these developmental levels are at one stage cognitively (or at least have been labeled that way) but this usually is not a reflection of their social/emotional levels. That's why keeping the approach to even simple songs pretty much the way you would with typical kids will work best. It honors their most intact creative/imaginative selves! I've worked extensively with children and young people and adults with disabilities and credit them all with teaching me a lot about what works!"

Stuart has worked with an organization called Very Special Arts (VSA), writing some sections on music in its "Start with the Arts" program.

Following are some of her pointers and strategies for using art to work with this very special population:

Arts and Learning for Students with Disabilities: Some Working Points for Best Inclusive Practices and Adaptive Strategies

1. Assume capable—leave your expectations at the door, and do not settle for other people's estimation of limitations. Always talk to the whole person/child, never to the disability. Keep in mind that there is no such thing as a disability that affects creativity. Expect to be amazed.

   However, get to know your students and what their needs and strengths are. Use your resources—physical, occupational, speech and other therapists; family members, peers, teachers and other specialists—for practical advice which will help make adaptive strategies work well for the student in your setting. You will get the most useful information if you are proactive and ask about the student in a positive way. Inquiring about the strengths and most effective learning strategies for a student will elicit the best information and get everybody off to a good start. Most of all—include the students themselves in the process of making adaptive strategies that work well for them. They may be their own best problem solvers.

   In the same vein, pass along information about the student in a positive way, being sure to highlight what's working well. A student may well be revealing her best potential in arts activities, and this is invaluable to others who work with her. If you need to let others know of difficulties, ask in terms of what could be improved, what would be a better approach?

2. Art is about choice—this is the basis of our work in the arts with all students, offering them the chance to make their own aesthetic choices, finding ways to offer those opportunities and honoring their choices.

3. Art is about problem solving—what color will go well here, what sound will make this piece even better, what movement will show how smooth water is. Students with disabilities are supreme problem solvers. They have to be because things which those without disabilities do automatically, they have to think through and work at, so art is the perfect place to tap those talents.

4. There are no right or wrong ways to do art. It is in art that unique ways of expressing oneself and experimental and unorthodox ways of executing that expression are highly valued. This makes it the perfect arena for individuals with disabilities…to excel and exhibit their greatest abilities.

Stuart also highlights art's potential as a valuable learning tool for all students, one that can be used to link creative activities to goals, benchmarks and standards in academic and life-skill areas. Understanding a subject in multiple ways demonstrates a deeper knowledge of what has been learned. She goes on:

5. Communicate, communicate—talk it over—especially with the individual involved. Never talk about the student in her or his presence without asking permission or at least explaining to them that you are going to be talking with another person to find a good way for them to do the activity. Find out what communication systems are in place for learners who are non-verbal or who have limited communication. If the student's communication system is not serving well in the project you are doing, problem solve and try new ideas.

I have seen artists develop new communication techniques which were then adapted by parents and teachers and the student's speech pathologist!

In talking about a student's art, use "I messages." Telling a student that a painting is wonderful, no matter how well-intentioned, is a judgment. Perhaps the student [may think] that it is not really the best they can do. They then may think, "Oh well, I guess I do not have to try harder to make a better picture" or "Well, that is stupid—doesn't [she] see that I can do better?" Specific comments which reflect a teacher's observation, such as "I love the way you've made so many of your brush strokes swirl and dip—I see lots of movement in your painting" [are more effective]. Ask questions which get them to talk about the work such as, "Tell me about the shapes in the sky," rather than simply, "What is it?"

This is not to say that we do not instruct and lead students to stretch themselves and to learn new skills. There are times when you may want the student to simply experience and explore what is being offered. There are times when a student may be eager to learn something new. Passing judgment is not, however, the most effective way to do this. "Think about the sound of the triangle in this measure of music. How well does it fit in at this point? Is the bright sound best for this part of the composition?" Or even, "Try a softer sound there and see which you like best—and why!"

Open-ended questions are the key. It is helpful to practice and role-play this kind of conversation!

6. Always choose the lowest level of intervention when assisting. We are looking for the least restrictive ways for [a] child to participate. The goal is for the child to work as independently as possible. Be alert to improper hand-over-hand where the one assisting is actually doing the work, to over-direction, to taking away a child's choice, or to doing a child's work for her or him. Take the time to work out strategies that meet individual needs and allow as much independence as possible. There is always the temptation to do the work for a child, either to improve outcome or to speed things along. But if educators invest time up front to work out these strategies, in the end it will be both more expedient and more satisfying for both teacher and child.

7. Adaptive equipment—a few thoughts on fancy equipment versus clever uses of what is available: there are many new and exciting kinds of technology which are useful and effective. However, often this technology is either unaffordable or does not quite work, since all children are different. Use what works for the child, but remember that problem solving the need for each child can be done with whatever is at hand. Remember that as we are working as artists, problem solving is our greatest strength!

This last point is more applicable to classroom situations, but [it] has points worth thinking about for children in the hospital or with health care needs.

8. Adaptive approaches—an open environment is beneficial for all students. By this we mean experiences where students are offered a variety of materials and encouraged to explore different ways to participate in the activity or accomplish the end product. When children with disabilities are included in the group, thought will naturally

be given to accommodating their needs. It is highly important to be sure that whatever materials or approaches are included with particular students in mind are also available to everyone in the group. There is sometimes anxiety about the most able students choosing simpler ways of doing a project—but rest assured, this is never a problem! Quite the opposite will happen. All students will benefit from unique ways of approaching creative work. For instance, if a visual arts class includes a student with low vision and more tactile materials are included as an option, this may add a wonderful new dimension for all participants.

Remember that learning is a circular and not a linear process. There are always core goals for any activity we do with children—whether classroom, recreational, or arts activities. In dance, theater, music, and the visual arts the teacher will have a core aesthetic goal. But there are 360 degrees of ways to accomplish that goal. When we, as educators, allow the choices and process of exploration so that each child finds her or his unique way to experience the creative process, which will take them on a journey towards that core, we provide the most meaningful, satisfying and potentially successful opportunities for all students.

Stuart concludes, "I feel deeply that what all of us who do this work have to pay the most attention to is honoring what is whole in everyone. It's just too easy to think of what is 'different' or 'needed' and then design what we do with that in mind. We do need to tailor our approaches of intentions, but don't we do this with every program/workshop/performance/class we ever do! With the best of intentions, the approach to children—and particularly with young people and adults—with disabilities has been to cast about for what is 'simple enough for them to understand' when what I have learned (sometimes the hard way) is that all we need to do is look for common ground—ways of doing music, ways of being expressive which do suit the moment but which are completely satisfying for both music performer/leader/participant/audience."[3]

[3] I am extremely grateful to Deborah for permission to reprint this information. Thank you so much, Deborah. There is a whole world of dedicated folks out there who work exclusively with children with "special needs."

Read More about Families with Special Needs

Healthybooks: http://www.Healthybooks.org.

Heller, Sharon. *Too Loud, Too Bright, Too Fast, Too Tight: What to Do If You Are Sensory Defensive in an Over Stimulating World.* New York: Harper Collins, 2002.

"Music and Autism." *Early Childhood Connections: Journal of Music and Movement-Based Learning* 9, no. 4 (2003).

"Music for Children with Special Needs." *Early Childhood Connections: Journal of Music and Movement-Based Learning* 3, no. 2 (1997).

Notbohm, Ellen. *Ten Things Every Child with Autism Wishes You Knew.* Arlington: Future Horizons, 2005.

Nwokah, Eva. "Emergent Literacy for Children with Special Needs: Developing Positive Interest in Literacy Experiences." *ACEI Focus on Infants and Toddlers* 19, no. 1 (2006).

Roth, Froma P., Diane R. Paul, and Ann-Mari Pierotti, "Let's Talk: For People with Special Communication Needs." American Speech-Language-Hearing Association (ASHA), 2006. http://www.asha.org/public/speech/emergent-literacy.htm.

"Special Focus on Children with Disabilities." *Music Educators Journal* 92, no. 4 (2006).

VSA Arts: http://www.vsarts.org.

Read More about Children and Music

Angier, Natalie. "The Dance of Evolution; or, How Art Got Its Start." *New York Times,* November 27, 2007. http://nytimes.com/2007/11/27/science/27angi.html#.

Baney, Cynthia Ensign. "Music Makes a Difference."*Early Childhood News,* March–April 1999.

Coulter, Dee Joy. "Music and the Making of the Mind." *Early Childhood Connections: Journal of Music and Movement-Based Learning* 1, no. 1 (1995).

Heyge, Lorna L. Interview with Cynthia Ensign Baney. *Early Childhood Connections: Journal of Music and Movement-Based Learning* 2, no. 4 (1997).

Hornbach, C. "Ah-eee-ah-eee-ya-eee, Bum and Pop, Pop, Pop: Teacher Initiatives, Teacher Silence, and Children's Vocal Responses in Early Childhood Music Classes." Ph.D. diss., Michigan State University, 2005.

Neely, Linda Page, Susan Kenney, and Jan Wolf. *Start the Music, Strategies.* Reston, Va.: MENC, 2000. http://www.menc.org.

El Sistema: Changing Lives through Music. April 13, 2008. http://www.cbsnews.com/stories/2008/04/11/60minutes/main4009335.shtml.

Smith, Janice. "Every Child a Singer: Techniques for Assisting Developing Singers." *Music Educators Journal* 92, no. 4 (2006).

Taggart, Cynthia Crump. "Creating a Developmentally Appropriate Early Childhood Music Environment." *Michigan Music Educator* 45, no. 1 (2007).

"When to Begin Instrumental Lessons?" *Early Childhood Connections: Journal of Music-and Movement-Based Learning* 5, no. 4 (1999).

2

Family Sharing
A Trip Down Memory Lane

There was music in my mother's house.
There was music all around. . . .
There was music in my mother's house.
My heart still feels full with the Sound.
—Stuart Stott

No one says it better than the families I work with in my classes, who have experienced firsthand just how much music impacts their lives. I am eternally grateful for their time and for their willingness to share their stories.

A brand-new student's birth announcement included this poem:

Prayer for a New Baby
We are grateful for this new baby, who is small in body yet great in Soul, who has come into our midst as a gift.
May we be sensitive to the sacred as we nurture and learn from this child. Give us patience. Give us strength.
And grant us wisdom and love to help this child learn to sing her own song.
—Anonymous

One mom was on her way to class, bringing her two-year-old and her new three-month-old infant, after dropping her five-year-old at school. She felt frazzled and overwhelmed, as one can only imagine, and her two-year-old said, "It's okay, Mommy. Gari's music will make you feel better."

A parent of a five-month-old wrote me after her first class, "Oh, what a gift. Baby (judging from her smiles) and I can't wait to come back. I want to learn more about being there for your kids by not being the director, but merely an observer. I guess, we are here to sing and dance along with our children and that is it!"

A mom who has been coming for over five years with two children tells me, "You always remind me of the fundamental importance of peace and gentleness in our world."

The thrilled dad of a slow-to-warm-up eighteen-month-old, after ten short weeks of class, reported that the child now "runs through the house with toilet paper streamers singing 'Bim Bam.'"

The mom of two boys, ages three and a half and sixteen months, wrote after her very first class, "Thanks for a great music class today! You do a fabulous job! This class is exactly what I hoped for. I left today feeling great. Few things make me happier than making music with my children."

As I was finishing work on this book, I bumped into a mom who had long brought her three children, now ages five, eleven and fifteen, to my class. She said she remembers my studio "as a warm place downstairs, a roomful of strangers sharing intimate moments" with their children. She found it "a place of content, no pride, no ego, just peace and warmth."

In this spirit of family sharing, I want to mention that it is of special importance to remember that every child develops on her or his own timetable. I once heard it said that if we compare our children to one another, we will miss out on our own child's uniqueness.

Parent: At the time of each child's birth, make up a song for them, about four verses, and sing it every day. Each of my children recognizes [their song] with love every time I sing it.

A powerful connection for this mom, stated so simply.

Parent: My eighteen-month-old daughter rarely put herself out there in class, but would sing and move to the music the minute we got into the car.

This topic is a familiar one, frequently posed by my families. After just a few classes, a parent might say, "Johnny isn't doing anything! I want to drop out." I always encourage parents to stick with it. The child who seems not to be doing "anything" is often the one getting the most out of the program. This is the child who is participating via observing and listening. Listening is what it's all about, where it all begins: it's hard to make music without listening skills. So much in our society is visual that many children and adults don't have good listening skills, even though they're essential for learning and socialization.

This also speaks to individual learning styles, a key emphasis of my philosophy. Just as adults have different learning modes, young children do too. Some may need to watch or have visual cues or touch everything, while some just need to do-do-do. As teachers and parents, we must remember to honor these individual learning styles.

We all have high hopes for what our children will be like. More often than not, however, our children will turn out different from what we imagined or planned. When I was a young mom, the greatest lesson I learned was to accept my children for who they were and, more importantly, for who they were not. As parents, we want our children to actively participate in whatever we deem important. Letting go of this desire is often the hardest lesson for parents to learn. Many of my families tell me just how difficult it is to leave their expectations at the music school door—how difficult it is to let go for forty-five minutes a week, sit back, enjoy their children and let them experience making music in their own way.

If children don't have to worry about pleasing their grown-ups, they can concentrate and listen to the music. This empowers them, and it will go a long way toward enhancing their musical development, their emotional well-being and their self-esteem.

Once babies are past six months, unless they have special needs, I ask adults not to move their hands for them, as this may inhibit their self-expression or lead to a power struggle. Just as we would not open and close their mouths for our children to help them learn to talk, we usually don't need to tap their drum or shake their bells. One mom who attended every Thursday morning at the same time over nine years, with three sons, told me how hard it was for her to sit back and let her boys do their thing in whatever manner they chose. After tearfully leaving music class, as her youngest boy moved into kindergarten, she told me that it took her two years to get there and that it had an enormous impact on her parenting in general.

Parent: My fourteen-month-old, outgoing son did not speak clearly but was able to sing and sang lyrics much better than he was able to speak.

This is so often the case, language skills developing after musical skills, again reinforcing the fact that not all children learn in the same way. Some have receptive language (understanding) long before they actually speak.

Parent: My daughter, four and a half years old, is shy and cautious. Her social skills were very positively impacted through exposing her to music class these past few years.

Although I prefer "slow-to-warm-up" to "shy," as an educator I know that the social/emotional benefits of music are vital. We are so busy pushing academics, putting our little ones in front of computers and encouraging baby Yolanda to recite her ABCs, that we may overlook the importance of our children's social and emotional lives in the early stages of development.

When I worked in the classroom, I had a three-year-old who could read fluently but had no understanding of socially acceptable behavior, often hitting and striking out at the other children in frustration. This was in the early 1990s, before "Baby Einstein," yet parents were still requesting that I teach their two- and three-year-olds how to read and write. I did not know as much about the research and developmentally appropriate practice as I do now, but I did know that if children did not have good social skills—the emotional confidence to feel good about themselves and feel empathy for others—the traditional three Rs would be of little use to them. I took a stand and refused these parents' demands, saying that my job was to help socialize their children. Nevertheless, some fifteen years later, I still see society's emphasis on academics over children's social and emotional lives, even with infants, and it saddens me.

Parent (of a ten-month-old): We've been singing and playing music for him since before he was born. It always seemed to have a calming effect on him and us! We use it during diaper changes and at bedtime.

What a gift this family has given this child and themselves, beginning to expose him to music even before he was born. Music can be a caregiver's best friend. Using music to ease daily tasks makes these pleasant rituals for baby and parents, smoothing sometimes stressful situations. But the repetition of the music also helps the baby learn to feel safe and know trust.

Parent: We had no idea what an impact this class would have. Both of our daughters have gained an appreciation for all kinds of music and the confidence to express themselves through song and dance. They have developed more rhythm in their short lives than I have in all my thirty-five years! It is a real testament to the power of music when we witness our girls' excitement at a variety of musical events.

Parent: I am grateful for the opportunity to relearn songs I had long forgotten. As a child I remember sitting on a swing for hours as a time, just humming or making up words to my own songs. Now I watch my son (two years old) delight in playing with music by adapting tunes, phrases and rhythms we've learned in class. I had forgotten how wonderful singing is. It is amazing how musical a finger or a foot or a pretend whistle can be! Sadly, so many of these simple joys are lost in many families and replaced by the noise pollution of electronic toys and television.

Music has actually become another language in our home. Certain songs are shared for comfort, laughter and learning. Some of my son's favorite songs are in languages we don't speak. But he belts out the words without question and proves that music is a universal language. Music is so easily absorbed into the brain. From Gari's class we have come to appreciate music for its power to entertain, teach and bring joy to others. The format of her class keeps music fun and gives our son a great experience that will stay with him his entire life.

This parent said it all.

Parent: My older son, now almost four, had strong opinions about music before he was even born. When I was pregnant, I dutifully played classical music to my belly almost every day in my third trimester. I found it very tedious because I really didn't like classical music very much. He never moved a muscle when I played it. Finally, I couldn't take it anymore and I put on some Miles Davis. The baby was dancing on my pelvic bone in no time. Every time I put it on he would just start wiggling like a fish. I was in the car with my younger son, listening to Gari's music, when I heard a strange tapping sound coming from the backseat. I thought maybe something was wrong with his seatbelt. So I twisted around to see what was going on. There I saw my son, at five months of age, clapping to the music. And his timing wasn't really that bad either.

Gari has successfully identified a method of truly teaching music to babies and young children, not just playing music for them. Through her thoughtful deconstruction of songs, rhymes and sounds, my kids have started to comprehend the components of music, naturally, without any labels and on their own terms. Class has been a revelation of sorts for both of my kids. Watching their little minds expand from this experience has been a real gift for me.

Research supports the contention that hearing is the second sense developed in utero and that children will remember music they hear be-

fore they're born. I especially love this story, as it shows how some children establish preferences for a specific style of music at a very early age. Much commercially produced music for children is simply not good for them. It is too loud, too fast, too busy, too silly, too patronizing. It is so important to expose young children to all styles of music, but not just any music will do. It has to be appropriate and contribute to a rich musical environment. Some of the best music for children is not commercially available in stores. The resource section at the end of the book has some recommendations.

Parent: In Gari's program, she sings "bum, bum, bum, bum, bum…bum" [resting tone] and the children drop the instrument in the basket with the reply "bum." At home, my son starting doing this on his own. I started using this tune to clean up our toys at the end of the day. He loved putting things away in the toy basket, with a "bum." He was two years old at the time. Now, nine years later, my seventeen-month-old daughter is in the class and after just two months she is already responding to this same tune! We find adding a little music to our daily tasks makes us all feel good.

That's so much a part of what it's all about, taking the music home and making it a part of the daily routine. In this case not only are the children putting their toys away: they're learning tone and pitch, things that will stay with them throughout their lives. If they decide to play an instrument or sing in the choir, they will be that much more musically enriched from an early age. Music teachers love this.

Parent: My son had his holiday party at preschool and the kids performed a little music and movement program for the parents, which was just precious. However, I noticed that he was one of only a few kids in his class who was properly keeping time with the music while using wooden sticks, jingle bells and such (exactly the same kind of instruments we've always used in our class).

I kept silently thinking, "Thank you Gari! Thank you Gari!"

I'm the one who's grateful to the many families whose lives I have touched, inspiring them to make music-making a part of their time together.

Parent: My music experiences: I grew up in a Polish family and on Christmas Eve every year we would get together with my extended family for a special meal called Wigilia (pronounced vee-GEE-leeah). After the meal we would sit around the table and sing Christmas carols. One of my favorite ones was sung in Polish. It is called "Dzisiaj W Betlejem," or "Today in Bethlehem." Every year I would play my mom's record of it until I learned the words. It meant a lot to be able to sing with my aunts, uncles and grandparents. It is among one of the many special memories I have of being with my family on Christmas Eve that I cherish. We have a tape of my grandparents singing that song many years ago. To hear their voices singing brings back many happy times.

Gari's class: When I first took my son to class, I wasn't sure if he would get much out of it but I later found out that Gari teaches more than music to the kids and parents alike. He would cry when we left the library and he had to leave behind the puppets. At Gari's class, the children take a dolly in the beginning, then say goodbye to it and put them all in a basket. She also does this throughout class with various musical instruments. Just after a few classes, I noticed that my son no longer had trouble giving up the puppets at

the library. I guess he realized they would be there waiting for him the next time we came to the library.

Last year when my son was about nineteen months old and learning to talk he started picking up the words from the songs we sing in music class. One day after class he started singing "bim bam berry berry bam" in the car. I was amazed that he picked up those particular words!

Gari has come up to me several times with praise for him and is always encouraging to the other students and parents. She encourages parents to let the children participate in any fashion they wish and that their participation levels do not mean they are not learning. When they are ready they will speak, dance, and make gestures. My son tends to sit and intently watch what is happening around him. Gari assures me that his listening skills are developing and the movement will come in time. People are amazed by how well he speaks for a two-and-a-half-year-old. I attribute it to the many books we read, the songs we sing at his request and his exposure in music class.

Perfect ending to a perfect day…

Grandparent: I can't thank you enough for all the wonderful years (seven) my grandchildren and I spent on many a Tuesday morning with you learning new (and old) music! You even brought back songs I had learned when I was younger!! All the children talk about the times we spent with you. I also remember a lot of the mothers and fathers and other grandparents I met at your classes! We wish you all the best and continued success with new families finding you! They are in for a treat . . .

The treat is mine . . .

What's It All About?

Words make you think a thought. Music makes you feel a feeling.
A song makes you feel a thought.
—E. Y. Harburg

Can the impact of music be studied scientifically? And so what if it can? Isn't it enough that young children love to make music, were born to move and to learn through moving? Can't we just have fun and leave it at that? Yes, yes, of course, yes.

But!

With studies chockfull of compelling data, affirming just how good music is for young children, it is impossible for me to write about its value without looking at the research. I have always enjoyed music because it feels good, but now we know how good it is for us—just how grand it really is. I am not a scientist, and sometimes I find study methodologies complex, but the outcomes absolutely thrill me.

Our current emphasis on the ABCs, academic achievement and "leave no child behind" may have left many children flat on their behinds. With music, art and physical education often the first programs cut from the curriculum, perhaps this glance at research will arm adults with the facts necessary to support the relevance of music, the need for it in our children's schools. Preschool has in fact become kindergarten, and kindergarten first grade. Young children are being asked to read and write before their brains are

ready. How does this happen? Could it be we are robbing children of their childhood? Shouldn't childhood be a journey, not a race?

Musically Speaking…Experts Tell Us

In 1998, the Arts Education Partnership (AEP) cited the following guiding principles for the development of arts-based programs and resources for young children:

- Children should be encouraged to learn in, through and about the arts by actively engaging in the processes of creating, performing and responding to quality arts experiences, adapted to their developmental levels and reflecting their culture.

- Some research in this area reveals that children's art arises from children's play. The arts experience becomes a source of communication and interaction for children and adults.

- Arts activities and experiences, while maintaining the integrity of the artistic disciplines, should be meaningful to children, follow a scope and sequence, and connect to early childhood curriculum and appropriate practices. They also may contribute to literacy development.

21

- Young children need increasing competence and integration across arts disciplines, including words, gestures, drawings, paintings, sculpture, construction, music, singing, drama, dramatic play, movement and dance.

- The development of early childhood arts programs (including resources and materials) should be shared among arts-education specialists, practicing artists, early childhood educators, parents and caregivers, and the process should connect with community resources.

- Some research indicates that young children cannot participate in artistic activities without appropriate materials, sufficient time, adequate space and the opportunity to be engaged by adults. Different experiences result from a child's solitary explorations and the engagement in the stimulating process of creating art.

Children are active learners, drawing on direct physical and social experience, as well as culturally transmitted knowledge, to construct their own understandings of the world around them.

- Movement nourishes and stimulates the brain (Don Campbell).

- Music is learned in many of the same ways in which a language is learned (L. Chen-Haftek).

- Brain scans make it clear that the parts of the brain responsible for initiating and coordinating movement are active during music listening, even when people lie perfectly still (Daniel Levitin).

- Exposure to classical music can stimulate brain development and connections responsible for many kinds of learning (Northwestern University study).

- Combining language with movement increases cognition 90 percent (Pat Wolfe).

- Singing is the most effective way to "charge" our own batteries. It is also a means of communication that goes beyond language (Paul Madaule).

- Swinging, rocking, vestibular activity is related to the highest level of thinking (Joan Firestone).

- What makes us move makes us think—movement builds the framework for cognition and brain development (Jean Blaydes-Madigan).

- Singing and dancing have been shown to modulate brain chemistry, specifically levels of dopamine, the "feel-good" neurotransmitter (Daniel Levitin).

- Singing and listening to nursery songs, folk songs and jingles can extend and develop vocabulary and comprehension skills (Kantaylieniere Hill-Clarke and Nicole Robinson).

- Training the preschool child's listening requires a strong emphasis on activities such as listening to music, singing, talking, reciting, acting—activities which combine the use of sounds with body movements (Paul Madaule).

- Literacy learning occurs by children actively making music through singing, moving, playing instruments, improvising, composing and listening (Melanie M. Willmann).

- All seven intelligences investigated by Howard Gardner are used in the playing of a singing game (Alan Strong and Mary Ann Nolterick).

- When hands are activated, as in tapping or the use of rhythm instruments, there is more effective learning (Chris Brewer and Don Campbell).

- There is no such thing as knowing too many nursery rhymes….Their phonetic context is quite rich and they go a long way in shaping a child's listening (Paul Madaule).

The AEP gives the following examples of how these guiding principles can be put into practice through developmentally appropriate arts experiences for young children:

Meaningful arts activities for infants and toddlers

- Draw from the best and simplest elements of the visual and performing arts
- Are rich in language and centered around one-on-one interactions with a significant adult
- Reflect a child's environment and everyday life and develop these experiences into different art forms
- Are embellished with encouraging language from adults and can be a source of sensory stimulation
- Provide a balance of sensory stimulation (sounds, movement, etc.) that is sensitive to the child's cues and signals
- Reinforce early language and literacy skills as adults connect language to toddlers' activities
- Include adult interaction and repetition in response to a child's interests

Meaningful art activities for preschool children

- Allow for child-initiated choices and action within the arts activity
- Engage children in process-oriented activities to explore, create and reflect on their own art and their experiences in the arts
- Emphasize process over product
- Foster imagination and have their origins in children's play
- Initiate children into child-friendly and appropriate performance, presentation and audience roles

- Connect to children's experiences and knowledge
- Include repeated contact sessions with art forms(s), draw upon progressive opportunities for involvement, and provide links to real life
- Evolve from and encourage interest in children's literature
- Reinforce children's language and literacy development

Meaningful art activities in the early grades

- Reinforce child-directed opportunities of expression and exploration
- Engage children in creating, reflecting and presenting their own art in child-friendly environments and settings
- Build upon the curricular goals and sequential skills of each artistic discipline and make interdisciplinary connections with learning across subject areas
- May lead to performance or presentation of children's artwork when they are socially, emotionally, physically and developmentally ready
- Emphasize the process of learning the arts and are not solely dependent on finished products

The AEP report further recommends assisting parents and other caregivers in understanding the importance of the arts, the role of the arts, and the design and implementation of activities that foster children's creativity, expression and physical and language development.[4]

As noted above, even though numerous studies suggest that music helps children focus on the structure of sounds, an important aspect in language development, music classes are often among the first to be cut when budgets are tight.

---

[4] This material is reprinted with permission of the Arts Education Partnership (AEP). The Arts Education Partnership is administered by the Council of Chief State School Officers and the National Assembly of State Arts Agencies through a cooperative agreement with the National Endowment for the Arts and the U.S. Department of Education. "Young Children and the Arts: Making Creative Connections" (1998) and "Children's Developmental Benchmarks and Stages: A Summary Guide to Appropriate Arts Activities" (2004) can both be accessed at http://www.aep-arts.org/publications/index.htm.

Parents and educators interested in bolstering their support of music programs in public schools should consider the following:

- Playing music can be good for your brain. A Stanford study found it helps the understanding of language.

- Early musical experiences can have major social benefits beyond language acquisition. According to Michael Blakeslee, of the National Association for Music Education, "If you want your child to be culturally literate, then you want him to study or listen to music."

- Nevertheless, according to the "National Assessment of Educational Progress," a study conducted by the Texas Department of Education, nearly one in five American schools fails to offer music or art classes even once a week.

Americans for the Arts (http://www.americansforthearts.org/), the nation's leading non-profit organization for advancing the arts in the United States, conducted a public-opinion survey and uncovered further pertinent results:

- Approximately 95 percent of parents believe the arts are important in preparing children for their future.

- Nonetheless, about 70 percent of parents feel that "someone else" is better suited to ask for increased arts education.

And consider the following statistics, from a survey commissioned by the International Music Products Association (http://www.texas-musicproject.org) and conducted by the Gallup Organization:

- More than 95 percent of respondents believe music is part of a well-rounded education.

- Approximately 71 percent believe that teenagers who play an instrument are less likely to have discipline problems.

- Close to 78 percent say learning a musical instrument helps you improve in other subject areas.

Americans for the Arts supports public perception of the importance of the arts in our schools, asserting that young people who participate in the arts for at least three hours, three days a week, for at least one year are

- Four times more likely to win an award for writing an essay or poem

- Four times more likely to be recognized for academic achievement

- Four times more likely to participate in a math and science fair

And Americans for the Arts goes even further, revealing music's broad and unexpected benefits:

- Preschoolers who were given music lessons improved their spatial-temporal reasoning.

- Elements of music and reading are highly related in first-graders. Those who participated in focused music listening had significantly higher reading scores.

- Brain scans taken during musical performances show that the entire cerebral cortex is active while musicians are playing.

- Early elementary children considered "emotionally disturbed" improved the quality and quantity of their writing when listening to music instead of writing in silence.

- At-risk first-graders who were taught basic letter and sound connections through movement showed more improvement than first-graders in the control group.

- Dance can help children discover the "music" of language.

- Dramatic play, rhyming games and songs are all language-rich activities that build pre-reading skills. Problems in learning to read could be prevented with early exposure to music, stories and books.

- Imaginative play helps kindergarteners make physical and social sense of their world.

- Creative drama improves learning-disabled students' behavior and language skills.

- Acting out stories benefits parents.

- In schools with strong arts climates, both teachers and students benefit.

To summarize, the arts

- Provide a cognitive use of the emotions

- Benefit teachers, parents and students

- Reach students in ways that they might not otherwise be reached

- Connect students to themselves and others

- Provide learning opportunities for the adults in the lives of young people

How much more do we need to know?

Read More about the Arts

Armistead, Elizabeth M. "Kaleidoscope: How a Creative Arts Enrichment Program Prepares Children for Kindergarten." *Young Children* (November 2007).

Campbell, Don. *The Mozart Effect for Children.* New York: William Morrow, 2000.

Campbell, Don, and C. Brewer. *Rhythms of Learning.* Tucson: Zephyr Press, 1991.

Chen-Haftek, L. "Music and Language Development in Early Childhood: Integrating Past Research in Two Domains." *Early Childhood Development and Care* (1997).

"Creativity." *Perspectives* (Winter 2007).

Dixon, Rozanne. "Orff-Schulwerk as Interdisciplinary Education: A Goldilocks Approach." *Orff Echo* (Winter 2008).

Greenberg, Day. "NU Study: Musical Training Helps Brain Process Sound." *Daily Northwestern,* March 29, 2007.

Hill-Clarke, Kantaylieniere, and Nicole Robinson. "It's As Easy as A-B-C and Do-Re-Mi: Music, Rhythm, and Rhyme Enhance Children's Literacy Skills." *Young Children* (September 2004).

Hunter, Tom. "Some Thoughts about Sitting Still." *Young Children* (May 2000).

"Learning through the Arts" (a curriculum-based program using the arts): http://www.ltta.ca.

Levitin, Daniel J. "Dancing in Your Seats." *New York Times,* October 26, 2007. http://www.nytimes.com/2007/10/26/opinion/26levitin.html.

Madaule, Paul. *When Listening Comes Alive: A Guide to Effective Learning and Communication.* Norval, Ont.: Moulin Publishing, 1994.

Strong, Alan, and Mary Nolterick. "Multiple Intelligences in the Music Lesson." *Kodaly Envoy* 22, no. 1 (1995).

Willmann, Melanie M. "An Investigation of Conceptual Congruencies between the Kodaly Method and Jerome Bruner's Instructional Theory." Ph.D. diss., University of Texas at Austin, 1983.

"Young Children and the Arts: Making Creative Connections." AEP, 1998. http://www.aep=arts.org/publications/index.htm.

PLAYMATE, COME OUT AND PLAY WITH ME

Play is the highest level of child development. It is the spontaneous expression of thought and feeling.
—Friedrich Froebel, *Education of Man* (1826)

A child is always above his average age, above his daily behavior in make-believe play and make-believe play contains all developmental tendencies in a condensed form and is itself a major source of development.
—L. S. Vygotsky (1996)

Play has always been the work of young children. But now children's play is in danger of becoming extinct. Recently, I received a catalog for pre-K publications featuring ideas for teaching children to play. Since when did children forget how to play? Why does teaching math and reading skills have to be connected to play? Play time is being replaced with structured activities, TV and computers. The push to standardize children has pushed recess off the playground. Children are literally being robbed of their childhood.

The American Academy of Pediatrics has stepped up to the plate with a study that points out how child-directed unstructured play is imperative for children's social, emotional and cognitive development, as well as for helping them deal with stress. "We are standing in the defense of play," says Kenneth Ginsburg, author of the report, which encourages children to save time to play—like children.

"The Importance of Play in Promoting Healthy Child Development and Maintaining Strong Parent-Child Bonds" cites various social forces that have continued to threaten play, including changes in family structure, competitive college-admissions processes, shorter recess periods and cuts in physical-education programs in many schools.[5]

The report's specific recommendations include:

- Emphasizing the use of "true toys" such as blocks and dolls, which allow children to fully use their imaginations, instead of toys requiring only limited imagination

- Helping parents evaluate claims by marketers and advertisers about products or interventions designed to produce "super-children"

- Encouraging parents to understand that each young person does not need to excel in multiple areas to be considered successful or prepared to compete in the real world

- Suggesting that families choose childcare and

---

[5] The AAP study on play can be found at http://www.aap.org/pressroom/playFINAL.pdf.

early education programs that meet children's social and emotional developmental needs, as well as prepare them for academic studies

The child-advocacy nonprofit organization Alliance for Childhood (http://www.allianceforchildhood.org) agrees with the study's results and has issued a "Call to Action on the Education of Young Children." Signed by more than 150 leading educators, physicians and other experts, the statement calls for a reversal of education policies that cut time for child-initiated play and emphasize formal instruction. Signers include Harvard professors Howard Gardner and Kathleen McCartney; pediatricians T. Berry Brazelton and Mel Levien; and child psychiatrists Kyle Pruett, Alvin Poussaint and Stanley Grenspan.

Michael K. Meyerhoff, of the Epicenter in Lindenhurst, Illinois, directs a family advisory and advocacy agency. He has also conducted research with the Harvard Preschool Project. In his presentation "The Power of Play," he further supports the benefits of play-based programs that give children a foundation for future learning. He reminds us that young children are physical creatures by nature. Play-based programs allow them to develop their natural inclinations to explore, investigate and experiment through developmentally appropriate play.

Meyerhoff suggests that by forcing academics into children's early years, we are merely "training" a child to mimic specific facts, because the child does not yet have the ability to truly understand the information. By putting young children in such purely academic situations, we are actually hurting them.

And the NAEYC concurs.

Sue Bredekamp and Carol Copple, for example, tell us that direct instruction may be totally ineffective: it is simply not attuned to a child's cognitive capacities and knowledge at such an early point in his or her development. Child-centered, child directed, teacher-supported play, on the other hand, is an essential component of developmentally appropriate practice.

Patricia Shehan Campbell and Carol Scott-Kassner assert that the skills acquired by children who initiate and direct their own learning are more relevant and useful in their lives.

And Elena Bodrova and Deborah Leong go even further, saying that children's play is not the opposite of work; rather, it *is* their work—"a form of social interaction that facilitates and mirrors the child's growing ability to engage in cooperative actions with peers." Bodrova and Leong also stress that early education expert Lev Vygotsky "believed that social context influences learning more than attitudes and beliefs, molding cognitive process, a part of the developmental process, with adults being a primary influence on a child's socialization process."

But today, en route to soccer and swim lessons, children can often be seen eating and doing homework in the car. When I walk around the neighborhood, I often find myself wondering, where are the children? Why aren't they outside playing? As a young child, I would go out after breakfast, run in for lunch and dinner and go back out until the street lights came on. Now children as young as twelve months are being plopped in front of computers.

Recently, I attended a symposium about the "vital importance of open-ended free play in children's lives," where the audience viewed the PBS documentary *Where Do the Children Play?* This film, which explores the power of creative play in the healthy development of young children, is simultaneously disheartening and encouraging. So, where are the children, and why aren't they playing outside? Some schools, the film reveals, now ban running, tag and dodge ball on the playground, while many have cut recess altogether. For many children, electronic media have become a substitute for play, depriving children of both self-exploration and the opportunity to learn how to engage with others. The film also compares the opportunities for play different children have—for example, the kind of play city children engage in versus the kind enjoyed by those from the suburbs.

After the screening of the documentary at the symposium, I had the privilege to meet with Joan Almon, who co-founded the nonprofit Alliance for Childhood in 1999 and is still its director. Featured in the film, she was kind enough to clarify some of its points for me.[6]

Film: Kids are not as healthy and will not live as long as their parents.… There are a complex of conditions and increase in drugs for psychological diseases.

Almon: I have heard a number of doctors say that they are concerned that today's children will have a shorter life expectancy than their parents. This is primarily due to the increase in childhood obesity and type-2 diabetes that eventually can also result in high blood pressure, increases [in] stroke and heart problems, etc. I have not seen this in writing in any official journal, however.

The other problem is that children show signs of increases in other physical disorders (allergies, asthma) and psychological problems (autism, bipolar disorders, depression), as well as hyperactive disorders. Growing numbers of children are on serious medications for these ailments, and the medications themselves often have side effects over time.

Because of this decline in children's health and well-being, the Alliance [for Childhood] was formed in 1999 to bring together educators and health professionals and others to address the underlying issues.

Film: Electronic media has become children's socialization and [leads to their] absorbing other people's creativity.

Almon: The average American child spends at least four hours per day in front of screens. Among the problems associated with this huge dose of media is that the children are continually absorbing other peoples' imaginations rather than developing their own. They are confronted with the creativity in others in such a way that it narrows their own creative outlets.

The media also robs them of time for socialization, for time in nature and for open-ended play.

Film: It is hard to define play; [the definition is] too long.

Almon: "Play" is so huge that it doesn't fit neatly into a definition. In this sense it is like "love," which also defies definition. In the UK, the play workers say, "It is a set of behaviors that are child-initiated, children-directed and intrinsically motivated."

Film: Play takes very little time. It lives at the heart and soul of every human being.

Almon: The spirit of play lives at the heart and soul of each human being, just as love does, and creativity. It is like a wellspring that continually renews itself. These are capacities or forces that last a lifetime, but sometimes we lose our access to them. It is as if there are many doorways leading to the chamber where they dwell, but the doorways get blocked with rubble. We can help children by preventing the rubble from entering

---

[6] Thank you to Joan Almon, not only for your generosity in clarifying these points for me but for all you contribute to the well-being of children and their families through the Alliance for Childhood.

or by clearing it if it is there. Sometimes even a small effort on our part allows the fountain of play to bubble freely again, and the children do the rest of the work.

Film: Give children a chance to create.

Almon: Children need time every day to be in touch with themselves and be creative. Sometimes we have to turn off the screens or limit the organized activities to give children a chance.

Film: In the business world, young workers often lack social skills. Play can help teach each other life lessons with a whole range of experiences coming into play.

Almon: In child-directed play, the children are continually communicating and negotiating with one another. They're creating and problem solving. Without play they tend not to develop these capacities well. We hear anecdotes from the business world that the young college graduates they hire now often lack these skills, and the corporations spend much time and money to help the young people to develop social capabilities.

Film: Children learn how to handle risk [by playing].

Almon: Life is full of risk, and the one thing we can be sure of is that children will encounter challenges during their lifetime. We only don't know how great the challenges will be, what kind they'll be or at what stage of life. But there is no way to protect children or adults from risk. What we can do is to help children learn to meet the natural risks inherent in play and being in nature. Children naturally risk-assess and generally know how far they can go without serious harm.

There are always exceptions, however. There are the "daredevils" who are often highly accident prone, and there are the overcautious children who don't take enough risks. But most children extend themselves and their skills by taking reasonable risks and mastering new challenges. Rather than creating play spaces that are "risk-free," it's best to create spaces that allow as much risk as is reasonable.

Film: Children's behavior will match our expectations. True self-esteem comes from play.

Almon: Children have a "genius" for play. They know what they want to play and need to play to resolve many of their life issues. When given a chance to exercise this genius, they develop a deep self-confidence. When it is continually denied, however, they grow up feeling that they don't know how to meet their own social and emotional needs or guide their own learning processes. We adults need to trust the unique genius of each child.

After the screening of the film, a distinguished panel took questions from the audience. One of the panelists was Lawrence Schweinhart, the president of High/Scope Educational Research Foundation.[7] He mentioned High/Scope's preschool study, which compared direct instruction to a play-based approach for preparing children for school. Schweinhart further distinguished between two different perspectives on education, one emphasizing learning about life and the other learning from a teacher.

Scheweinhart later clarified the study's conclusions for me, extending his points to include children's emotional well-being as well. "During their schooling," he said, "47 percent of the 'direct instruction' group, whose preschool program included no play, but only 6 percent of the

---

[7] My sincere thanks to Lawrence Schweinhart for his time and for all that High/Scope does to contribute to the well-being of young children and their families. A more complete description of the High/Scope Preschool Curriculum Comparison Study is available at http://www.highscope.org/Content.asp?ContentId=241.

High/Scope and nursery school groups, whose preschool program included play, required treatment for emotional impairment or disturbance. The difference in play between these groups is clearly shown by the fact [that] the 'direct instruction' classroom had no equipment and materials other than tables, chairs and a textbook, while the High/Scope and nursery school education is [focused on the idea] that children's learning comes from their experience with materials and other people."

The documentary also highlighted the important role nature plays in children's emotional and intellectual development. This point was frosting on the cake for me: a simple walk around the block, in the woods, by a river or at the lake brings instant stress relief, peace and calm. The film stresses the fact that all these things—things we crave for our children—are available for free, but so many things in our children's lives today separate them from nature rather than engaging them in it. Urban sprawl cuts out open outdoor space, with play becoming secondary. And children removed from nature are all too often removed from having a private life. Richard Louv, author of *Last Child in the Woods: Saving Our Children from Nature-Deficit Disorder,* remarks that we should replace "leave no child behind" with "leave no child inside." Louv speaks of the "abstract" notions available to us in nature, pointing out that this "generation is growing up looking at screens, which does not require using all their senses at one time—only in nature do we use all our senses at once." Addressing the notion of "stranger danger" as the number-one reason parents give for keeping their kids inside, he asks why we are "allowing fear to reorganize our lives." "I think," he concludes, "it's journalism"—the media again!—"that conditions us to live in a state of fear."[8]

The film ends with a quote from Einstein: "We cannot solve problems with the same thinking that created those problems," reassuring viewers that "it's not hard to bring children back to play." So turn off everything, and take your children by the hand to the park, to the woods, to the river. Take no toys, and see what adventures await you. It will change your outlook and may even change your life.

When the Trees Sing

When the trees sing, it doesn't really matter
If you know the song,
Or if you know the words,
Or even if you know the tune.
What really matters is knowing
That the trees are singing at all.
—Mattie Stepanek

Children need time to play with each other and to direct their own play. Kenneth Ginsburg emphasizes the fact that studies show that when children get a play break, their brains store academic information better. Children at play also learn social skills—how to negotiate, who goes first, what's fair, what's not. Parents can even join in; they just can't run the show, Ginsburg says. When the parents take direction, they become more connected with their kids.

Regardless of how innocent our help may appear or feel, when we interrupt a child's play, we interrupt their process, and they will often walk away. The media tells parents they will be letting their children down if they do not keep up with the push to put technology into the crib. How lucky the children whose parents, caregivers and grandparents let them play, without pressure, expectations or interference.

In our world of media guidance and technological pressure, just letting children be is now a rare commodity. Isn't third grade soon enough

---

[8] Read more about Richard Louv, his philosophies and his book at http://www.grist.org/news/maindish/2006/03/30/louv/.

to learn how to use a computer? Many children in kindergarten now have forty-five minutes in their curriculum allotted to the computer lab and twenty minutes to art. Can this possibly be in the best interests of young, developing minds and bodies?

The Role of Play

Children do not just play: they live in and through their playing, with a capacity for total flexibility—both here and now and beyond time and space. Children are what they play. It is through play that they build new highways into the unknown—including, when necessary, regions that lie beyond the here and now.

—Jon-Roar Bjorkvold, "The Music Within: Creativity and Communication, Song and Play"

In the article "The Role of Play in Early Childhood Education," Kathleen Jacobi-Karna gives us a historical perspective on play. The concept, she tells us, was first introduced as "an integral part of the young child's learning process in the 1600." Taking account of the history of play can reveal where we have been and where we are going. If we had it so right, how did it go so wrong?

Jacobi-Karna's survey begins with the Czech educator Jan Amos Comenius (1592–1670). Although Comenius is now considered the father of modern education, some of his beliefs, such as his emphasis on lifelong learning and the importance of education for all, were not held in high regard by his contemporaries. Comenius, Jacobi-Karna tells us, "supported creating a separate curriculum for young children from infancy to six. Within this curriculum, play was a necessary component of the learning process." Imagine that!

Jean-Jacques Rousseau (1712–1778) stressed that early childhood education should give

children time to be children, not to prepare for adulthood. "He believed," Jacobi-Karna remarks, "education should be in a natural setting, with limited adult intervention—his concept of discovery learning."

The Swiss educator Johann Heinrich Pestalozzi (1747–1827) shared the idea that a natural setting provides the best stage for play-based learning. Pestalozzi believed that "experience and self-discovery were primary modes through which children learned. He believed that for the young child, 'work and play are all one for him, his games are his work; he knows no difference.'"

Friedrich Froebel (1782–1852), a German educator known "as the founder of kindergarten," "placed music at the heart of early childhood education," Jacobi-Karna tells us. "Play," he believed, "served as an integral avenue for children's learning.…His 'gifts' of balls, cylinders and cubes and 'occupations' of constructive play experiences are considered by some as the first educational materials."

The Swiss psychologist Jean Piaget may be the most familiar to many of us. Piaget's theory of cognitive development detailed the types of play that are dominant during each cognitive stage. Jacobi-Karna lists them:

- Practice play: repetitive actions, sensorimotor stage [birth—two years]
- Symbolic play: make-believe and imaginative; peroperational stage [two—seven years
- Games with rules: concrete operational stage [seven—eleven years]

The Reggio Emilia approach, developed by Loris Malaguzzi (1920–1994), may also be familiar to many of us. This approach is not considered a method. Rather, the curriculum emerges from the interests of the children, negotiated and created by teachers and children together. Stacie Goffin and Katherine Wilson list the characteristics of the Reggio Emilia "image of the child":

- The child is to be respected for his or her intellect and feeling instead of from the point of view of, "what part or parts of this child do we need to fix?"

- The "here and now" is paramount—what the child needs at this moment in time—as opposed to regarding early childhood education as a preparation for later education.

- The child is a participant and contributor to a social and cultural community.

- The child has multiple ways—100 languages—to express his or her knowledge and awareness.

All aspects of positive development are affected by play. "Through play," Jacobi-Karna explains, "children learn to function as part of a group, developing socially and cognitively. Creative expression through play is considered one of the '100 languages' through which young children express their understanding of the words. Physical skills such as fine and gross motor are developed through play experiences."

NAEYC position statements on developmentally appropriate practice (DAP) support the notion of the vital role play takes in children's development:

- Children should have opportunities to play together: it enhances their development and learning.

- Children should have extended blocks of time for playing and undertaking projects.

- Children benefit both from self-initiated spontaneous play and from teacher-planned and -structured activities and experiences: incorporating play into learning is not an either/or, but a both/and proposition.

The Music Educators National Conference (MENC) concurs:

- [Musical] experiences should be integrated within the daily routine and play of children.

- Musical experiences should be play-based and planned for various types of learning opportunities, such as one-on-one, choice time, integration with other areas of the curriculum, and large-group music focus.

- A music curriculum for young children should include many opportunities to explore sound through singing, moving, listening, and playing instruments.

- Children's play is their work. Children should have opportunities for individual music play, such as in a "music corner," as well as for group musical play, such as singing games. Children learn within a playful environment. Play provides a safe place to try on the roles of others, to fantasize and to explore new ideas. Children's play involves imitation and improvisation.

Jacobi-Karna, in her overview of the history of play, asks, "What can we do to promote play in the music education of young children?" And she makes some clear suggestions:

- Create an environment conducive to supporting play—a physical space and materials. Also, [it's] important to provide unconventional instruments or music makers, since in the hands of a child every object is capable of producing a sound and becoming an instrument.

- Provide opportunities to play/explore and with various types of interaction. [There should be] time for children to work in small groups and individually. Children should have a voice in determining the makeup of smaller groups.

- Make the teacher's role to facilitate, question, and co-create.

Jacobi-Karna cites Elizabeth Wood and Jane Attfield in further describing the adult's role in play. The adult, she tells us, should focus on:

- Supporting and responding to children's needs and potential

- Supporting children's skills as players and learners

- Enriching the content of [children's] play

- Supporting [children's] own ideas and providing additional ideas and stimuli

- Enabling children to elaborate and develop their own themes

- Being responsive to the level of play development

- Remaining sensitive to the ideas that children are trying to express

In conclusion, Jacobi-Karna asserts that providing time to play may be "one of the most challenging aspects" of our lives as parents and educators. Addressing the question of what might be an adequate amount of time, she suggests that "it may make sense to take the music educator to the children and assist the classroom teacher in providing music materials that can be accessed at any given time—not just on Wednesdays from 10–10:30.…Instead of asking what young children need in order to be successful later, maybe it is better to ask what children need right now. Clearly," she says, "they need time to play." Bravo to the author: we can all learn many lessons from her.

More than Child's Play

In *Education of Man,* published in 1823, Friedrich Froebel tells us that play reveals the child's inner life in an outward form. Walter Drew, of the Institute for Self-Active Education, supporting Froebel's views, explains that adults who work and play with children create a genuine bond with them—a bond that promotes mutual respect. Froebel, Drew tells us, advocated less interference with children's living and learning: all people, including children, are more receptive if they cooperate by choice, rather than through coercion.

Only the child's self-activity—his or her own actions—leads to true understanding. In the space of self-active play, there is peace, excitement and inspiration. Wisdom unfolds. And Drew believes that these broad, vital results can be encouraged through the simplest of objects: building blocks and recycled materials. In creative play with blocks, Drew says, we reaffirm our capacity to create harmony and order, our inner power to express thought through active construction. Children and adults all benefit from such creative play and contemplation: we are the producers of our own knowledge.

Building with blocks: what a simple, inexpensive concept. And what a far cry from pushing buttons, from toys that tell our children what to do, think, feel! And today such toys are even being marketed for infants. Where will it end?

Block play and self-active education, according to Walter Drew, works quite differently, developing:

- The capacity of expansion, elaboration, imagination, wideness of vision, as well as the ability to reason with compassion, complexity and richness. . . .

- The ability to organize ideas around an inspiring or higher ideal, or supremely luminous ideas or vision that will serve as a guide throughout life. . . .

- Self-control of the mind, that is, the ability to control one's own mind, to direct attention in a positive direction and to remain detached from troublesome thoughts, or negative influences. . . .
- Mental silence, perfect calm, so that we are more receptive and readily available to inspiration arising from deep within our heart and soul. . . .

According to researchers Farveh Ghafouri and Carol Anne Wien, when children play together, their play is complex. Play, as Brian Sutton-Smith reminds us, is never "just play....Play is the primary means of engaging in the world, and it provides children with a situation through which they can explore the world as it is, or the world as they imagine it. Social play is reciprocal. Social play is the mode that allows children to practice various social mores, such as taking initiative, solving problems, negotiating social relationships, taking turns and collaboration."

Playing Old Games

Archetypal games are quite simple and have the basic elements that children see in a play activity—an exercise for the body and the mind, and a surprise that makes them laugh.
—Sofia Lopez-Ibor, "Playing the Old Games"

Traditional children's games are a natural expression of music and dance, according to Sofia Lopez-Ibor. She tells us that through traditional games, "children discover the art of playing, as well as develop social and group skills, creativity and sensibility." Lopez-Ibor's lifelong project of collecting traditional games takes us from "Egyptian hieroglyphics to Renaissance murals

and Andean rugs, from paintings in Madrid to the Met in New York. [In all these places] you can find curious representations of children at play....Artists have captured children in doing what they most want to do: play games." She goes on to explain that "folk art around the world depicts children at play, galloping on hobbyhorses (made of banana tree leaves in one version), rolling hula hoops, juggling, shooting marbles and playing hide-and-seek."

Reminding us that many children no longer have opportunities for such fun and exploration, she describes this state of affairs as "tragic." "Children of the 21st century," Lopez-Ibor tells us, "are inheriting an impoverished culture from their elders. Traditional games are now mostly conserved in areas where the influence of the media culture is not so strong."

With fifth-graders, Lopez-Ibor created a get-acquainted project at the beginning of the school year that used the painting *Kinderspiele,* by Pieter Brueghel, which portrays customs from a sixteenth-century Flemish village. In this painting, she points out, there are more than two hundred children playing in the streets, on a "wonderful playground" where children ride on a barrel; walk on stilts; ride piggyback; carry each other; guess hands; somersault; play leapfrog, tug-of-war, and blind man's bluff. Lopez-Ibor calls this painting a "visual encyclopedia of games," featuring hula hoops, marbles, jacks, tops, dice, soap bubbles, hobbyhorses, hats, masks, capes, skirts to dance with, dolls, mud pies and fences to swing on.

In her classroom exercise with the fifth-graders, Lopez-Ibor pointed out that the painting depicts children playing more in the sixteenth century than they do now. One student responded, "We don't know how to be children anymore."

How is it that children no longer have time to play? Who let this happen? Lopez-Ibor wants to show us children's games with children themselves at the center. "Little by little," she laments, "all over the planet, folk traditions are being destroyed by social development and civilization. Recorded music and TV displace oral traditions. Computer games and modern toys substitute for traditional street games."

Lopez-Ibor's article saddened me, but it also gave me hope. It is not too late to turn back the hands of time. Educators and parents must rein in technology and bring back playtime for children. "Playing games," Lopez-Ibor reminds us, "is the children's culture....The schoolyard and the playground represent the field where games are transformed, where children create a new culture. Games are a way of learning and developing intellectual, physical, social and moral potentials."

Musical Play

Barbara O'Hagin, who runs the music lab at Central Michigan University, suggests "musical play in early childhood programs is rarely implemented." The majority of early childhood music practitioners instead commonly employ a teacher-directed and -controlled instruction style (sometimes referred to as "circle time") with a large group.

This has always presented a personal struggle for me. I know that children learn best through child-directed and child-centered activities, but how does a group of toddlers "run the show"? Educators and parents must find ways to encourage guided exploration and improvisational play both in the classroom and at home.

In her music lab, O'Hagin helps pre-service teachers learn about music play centers and discovery learning. She models how to expand and stretch the lesson plan to include children's own musical decisions. For her, "the rules of the game can change at any time....We follow their lead and allow for a free flow and exchange of ideas

as warranted by the situation...honoring their creativity and decision making." These opportunities for children to contribute their own ideas and make the activity their own can clearly be carried over into the home, possibly creating a more harmonious environment.

O'Hagin's work serves as an inspiring model for programs all over the country. Her goal is "to create conditions for learning that will benefit a child's music creative imagination leading to self-expression....We need to honor children's own ideas, inventions, and expressions, and allow them to grow."

So let's give our children lots of unstructured indoor and outdoor time for play—with blocks, music, drama and art; solo and with other children. Does your daycare or preschool have a play-based program and leave computers out of the picture for now? Make time to play with your children at home. Again, shouldn't childhood be a journey, not a race?

We must remain as close to the flowers, the grass and the butterflies as the child is who is not yet so much taller than they are. Whoever would partake of all good things must understand how to be small at times.
—Friedrich Nietzsche

Read More about Nature and Children

Erickson, Martha Ferrell. "The Children and Nature Network: Ensuring That All Children Can Spend Quality Time Outdoors." *Journal of the National Association for the Education of Young Children* (January 2008). http:www.journal.naeyc.org/btj/200801/BTJNatureErickson.asp.

Hoisington, Cynthia. "Let's Find Out about It! 'Doing Science' in Preschool." *Early Childhood News* (January–February 2006).

Louv, Richard. *Last Child in the Woods: Saving Our Children from Nature-Deficit Disorder.* New York: Algonquin Books, 2005.

"Nature in Children's Lives: Early Childhood Connections" (numerous articles). *Early Childhood Connections: Journal of Music and Movement-Based Learning* 5, no. 3 (1999).

Rosenow, Nancy. "Teaching and Learning about the Natural World." (January 2008). http://www.journal.naeyc.org/btj/200801/BTJNatureRosenow.asp.

Where Do the Children Play? Documentary and educational materials. Michigan Television, 2008. http://www.wfum.org/childrenplay/index.html.

Wilson, Ruth A. "The Wonders of Nature" Honoring Children's Ways of Knowing." *Early Childhood News* (January–February 2006).

Read More about Play

"Boundless Meanderings: To Play or Not Play." February 16, 2008. http://www.boundlessmeanderings.wordpress.com/2008/02/16/to-play-or-not-play/.

Bredekamp, S., and C. Copple, eds. *Developmentally Appropriate Practice in Early Childhood Programs Serving Children from Birth through Age Eight.* Rev. ed. Washington, D.C.: National Association for the Education of Young Children, 1997.

"Early Years Are Learning Years." http://www.naeyc.org/resources/eyly/1998/20.htm.

Elkind, David. *The Power of Play.* Cambridge: Da Capo, 2007.

Fluegelman, Andrew. *The New Games Book.* Garden City, N.Y.: New Games Foundation, 1976.

Ghafourt, Farveh, and Carol Anne Wien. "Give Us Privacy: Play and Social Literacy in Young Children." *Journal of Research in Childhood Education* 19, no. 4 (2005).

Goffin, Stacie G., and Katherine S. Wilson. *Curriculum Models and Early Childhood Education: Appraising the Relationship.* 2nd ed. Upper Saddle River, N.J.: Prentice-Hall, 2001.

Goodenough, Elizabeth. *Secret Spaces of Childhood.* Ann Arbor: University of Michigan Press, 2003.

"In Defense of Play." *Mothering Magazine* (January–February 2007).

Jacobi-Karna, Kathleen. "The Role of Play in Early Childhood Education." *Orff Echo* (Fall 2007).

Jenkinson, Sally. *The Genius of Play: Celebrating the Spirit of Childhood.* Stroud, U.K.: Hawthorn Press, 2004.

Read More about Play (continued)

Kessler, Crysta. "Play Is Child's Work." *Mothering Magazine* (May–June 2005).

Linn, Susan. *The Case for Make Believe: Saving Play in a Commercialized World.* New York: New Press, 2008.

Lopez-Ibor, Sofia. "Playing the Old Games." *Orff Echo* (Fall 2007).

Meyerhoff, Michael K. "The Power of Play: A Discussion about Early Childhood Education." Brochure. Lindenhurst, Ill.: Epicenter Inc.

National Association for Music Education. "Position Statement on Early Childhood Education."

Paley, Vivian Gussin. *A Child's Work: The Importance of Fantasy Play.* Chicago: University of Chicago Press, 2004.

"Planet Earth Playscapes": http://www.earthplay.net.

"Play." *Perspectives* (Spring 2007).

Riley, Jeanetta G., and Rose B. Jones. "When Girls and Boys Play: What Research Tells Us." *Childhood Education* (Fall 2007). http://findarticles.com/p/articles/mi_qa3614/is_200710/ai_n21100551.

Singer, Dorothy, and Jerome Singer. *The House of Make-Believe: Children's Play and the Developing Imagination.* Cambridge: Harvard University Press, 1990.

Sutton-Smith, Brian. "Conclusion: The Persuasive Rhetoric of Play." In *The Future of Play Theory: A Multidisciplinary Inquiry into the Contributions of Brian Sutton Smith,* ed. A. D. Pelligrini. Albany: State University of New York Press, 1995.

"Taking Play Seriously." *New York Times Magazine,* February 17, 2008. http://www.nytimes.com/2008/02/17/magazine/17play.html?ref=science&pagewanted=all.

Walter F. Drew Institute for Self-Active Education. "Froebel's Wisdom and the Wonder of Block Play." http:www.reusableresources.org/about.html.

Wood, Elizabeth, and Jane Attfield. *Play, Learning and the Childhood Curriculum.* 2nd ed. London: Paul Chapman Publishing, 2005.

Organizations That Promote Creative Play

Alliance for Childhood: http://www.allianceforchildhood.org, and http:www.allianceforchildhood.org/pdf_files/restoring_play_resources_110506.pdf.

Center for Creative Play: http://www.cfcp.org.

Children and Nature Network: http://www.cnaturenet.org.

Children's Environment's Research Group: http://web.gc.cuny.edu/che/cerg/.

Hooked on Nature: http://www.hookedonnature.org.

National Institute for Play: http://www.nifplay.org.

Natural Learning Initiative: http://www.naturalearning.org.

North Carolina Arts for Health Network: http://www.ncartsforhealth.org/Links.htm.

Play Wales: http://www.playwales.org.uk.

Playborhood: http://www.playborhood.com.

Sierra Club: http://www.sierraclub.org/youth/blog.

True Teachers: http://www.trueteachers.com.

U.S.A. Affiliate of the International Play Association: http://www.ipausa.org.

Wild Zone: http://www.wild-zone.net.

Zero to Three: http://www.zerotothree.org.

Read More about Musical Play

Berger, Audrey A., and Shelly Cooper. "Musical Play: A Case Study of Preschool Children and Parents." *Journal of Research in Music Education* 15, no. 2 (2003).

Chee-Hoo, Lum. "Children's Musical Surroundings: What Can Children Tell Us about Music Education?" *Orff Echo* (Summer 2007).

Chooi-Theng Lew, Jackie, and Patricia Shehan Campbell. "Children's Natural and Necessary Musical Play: Global Contexts, Local Applications." *MENC Journal* (May 2005).

Heath, Carol Quimby, ed. *The Song Garden.* West Hartford, Conn.: Kodaly Musical Training Institute, University of Hartford, 1986.

Levitin, Daniel J. "Dancing in the Seats." *New York Times,* October 26, 2007. http://www.nytimes.com/2007/10/26/opinion/26levitin.html.

Loong, Chet-Pang. "Early Childhood Music: Materials and Activities: Criteria and Guidelines for Selecting and Using Materials in Early Childhood Music Lessons." *OAKE-Kodaly Envoy Journal* (Summer 2007).

Neely, Linda Page, Susan Kennedy, and Jan Wolf. *Start the Music Strategies.* Reston, Va.: MENC, 2000.

O'Hagin, Isabel Barbara. "Children and Musical Play: Why Instructional Approach Matters in Early Childhood Music." *Michigan Music Educator* 45, no. 1 (2007).

Scott, Julie. "Pease Porridge Hot: Lesson Idea." *Reverberations: Orff-Schulwerk* (Spring 2007).

Stouffer, Mary. "Emotional Growth through Musical Play." Child and Family Canada. http://www.cfc-efc.ca/docs/cccf/00015_en.htm.

Van Der Linde, Ch. "The Relationship between Play and Music in Early Childhood: Educational Insights." *Education* 119, no. 4 (1999).

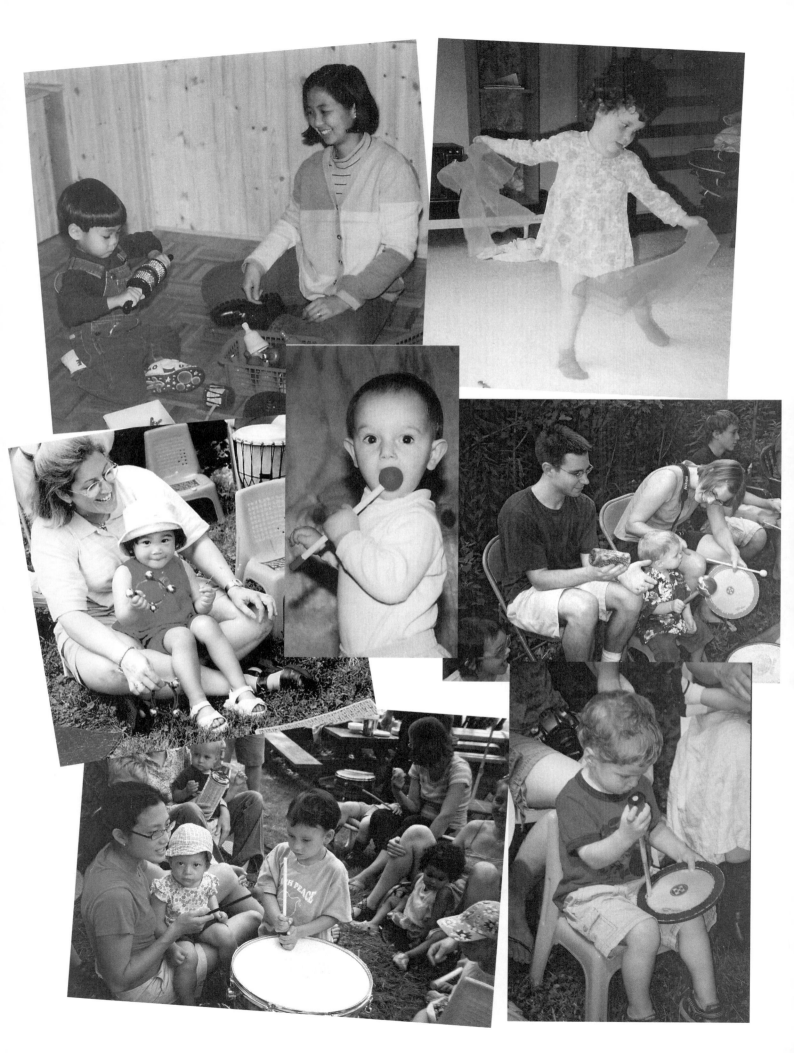

Music, Language and Literacy

Music is the language of the spirit. It opens the secret of life bringing peace, abolishing strife.
—Kahlil Gibran

Where words fail, music speaks.
—Hans Christian Anderson (1805–1875)

What a thrill for parents to hear the first sounds from their healthy, developing babies. I often wonder when, how, where language begins. I also think about babies who don't have language, for a variety of complex reasons, and how difficult this must be for new parents as well as baby.

As a grandmother and educator, I see sounds and language in terms of flow and rhythm, their onset tied to the relationship between a little one and his or her significant caregiver, beginning well before birth. How fortunate for caregivers to share this bath of sound!

The word "motherese" refers to the manner in which new parents speak to their infants, often using a higher and exaggerated pitch, slower tempos, larger or simpler contours. This special way of communicating enhances the musicality of language. Along with emotional and tactile cues, motherese is paramount in the acquisition of language.

Researchers W. Condon and L. Sandler from Boston University, for example, found out that infants' body movements were synchronized with the language sounds they heard. And Paul Madaule, of the Listening Centre, says that children play their bodies as musicians play their instruments. "The body," he explains, becomes the "language instrument." Think about this: how many young children talk to you standing perfectly still?

First come the sounds, and we echo back; then the words, and we echo back; then the sentences, and we echo back. Then perhaps follows what Jean Piaget termed "magical thinking"—a magical language that brings children into their all-important make-believe world.

Eric Miller writes, "as infants and toddlers attempt to speak, they are searching for means to communicate." Learning through imitation, they enjoy "words that are composed of sounds that echo and imitate the thing being represented—ting-ling-ling, cock-a-doodle-do, cuckoo....The child's verbal development is stimulated by having her communicative efforts responded to by caregivers." Children, Miller says, "play for the aesthetic pleasure of making rhythm rhyme, and other forms of repetition and pattern; and of making openings and endings, which give experience [of] form and closure."

The latest trend in TV programming for children, however, unfortunately might lead many parents to believe television is good for babies and might help them develop language. Miller, citing the work of Patsy Lightbrown and Nina Spada, refutes the value of such programming: "One-to-one interaction gives the child access to language which is adjusted to her level of comprehension. The response of the adult may allow children to find out whether their utterances are understood or not. Television does not provide such interaction. Even in children's programs, where simpler language is used and topics are relevant to younger viewers, there is no immediate adjustment for the needs of the individual child at each unique moment."

Verbal play is what helps children develop their language, through sounds, rhymes and melodies. *Teaching Music* magazine tells us, "when children learn to listen carefully while singing and playing instruments, they are learning to attend to sound, which will help immeasurably in their speech development."

John Gabrieli, a former Stanford University psychology professor, describes a study that demonstrated that "there's a specific aspect of language…that's changed in the minds and brains of people with musical training." Paul Madaule advises that as children have more developed language skills, we should "let them talk to themselves, make up words for the songs they sing, tell silly stories or produce all kinds of weird sounds."

Sonya Gruszczynski, a speech-language pathologist from Highlands Ranch, Colorado, points out that "early music classes are wonderful for facilitating early language development." She describes nursery rhymes and chants as wonderful connectors to language, the repetition of songs facilitating language comprehension. We know that receptive language comes before expressive language: when parents sing to their babies, then, they are giving them their daily dose of language comprehension.

In an exciting study conducted by Northwestern University, researchers found that early musical experiences even enhance long-term language learning in adults. "Musical experience improves the brain's ability to make sense out of the information it gets from your ear," says Nina Kraus, the director of Northwestern's Auditory Neuroscience Laboratory and the senior author of the study. Children's active engagement in music, in other words, will support their language development for the rest of their lives.

Young children, of course, don't know about the data; infants simply innately respond to the musical aspects of language. Janet Greene tells us, for example, that "the newborn demonstrates preference for the mother's voice through movement, suggesting that movement, music and language are integrated in the early development." Indeed, children naturally integrate speech, music and movement throughout their busy day. Greene finds that this integration highlights the shared components of music and language. Infants, she tells us, "may be using the phonological or musical elements of 'motherese or baby talk' to begin segmenting the language stream into meaningful units."

Greene reaffirms the importance of motherese, especially the impact of rhymes and songs in enhancing the musical elements of speech through slower tempos, longer pauses between phrases and an emphasis on dynamics. Greene thus reaches three conclusions:

- Songs and rhymes help develop oral language.

- Songs and rhymes integrate with movement to create a bridge from oral language to written language.

- The method of teaching music that allows children to sing, dance and chant (as in the Orff Schulwerk approach) belongs in the language-arts curriculum.

Cynthia Ensign Baney, whose research is based on the work of Dee Joy Coulter, likewise concludes that "the language development opportunities provided by songs and fingerplays are vital in the development of self-management."

Researcher Maryann Harman also shares some wonderful information, referring to Howard Gardner's notion of "multiple intelligences," explaining that music is the first of these "intelligences" "to become functional in a person." Gardner writes that "the single most important thing in education is for each person to find at least one thing that he/she connects to, gets excited by, feels motivated to spend more time with." Harman concurs and points out that "for many children music is that thing."

Working with very young children, Harman "noticed how syncopated rhythms were absent from their vocabularies, e.g., Winnie the Pooh becomes WinPoo." She wondered "if…tapping out these words in straight rhythms…might help them hear the entire word better. Using rhythm sticks or hands, the child says each sound of the word—Wi Ni the Pooh." Her approach seemed to work, "Parents were reporting that the children are speaking words they were having difficulty with after sounding them out in this fashion."

Music also gives us a chance to reconnect with the past, with traditions that were important in our own families of origin. I had the privilege of studying with John Feierabend, a foremost expert in the field of early childhood music, when I first began "Music for Little Folks," in the early 1990s. Feierabend recommends folk songs for children because of their "marriage of words and music where the melody emerges naturally from language." This part of Feierabend's mission—his emphasis on preserving traditional folk music—has helped form the foundation of my own program.

Music and Literacy

Two and two are four
Four and four are eight
Eight and eight are sixteen
Sixteen and sixteen are thirty-two.

Inchworm, inchworm, measuring the marigolds,
You and your arithmetic, you'll probably go far.
Inchworm, inchworm, measuring the marigolds,
seems to me you'd stop to see how beautiful they are.
—Hans Christian Anderson

In the early 2000's "The Mozart Effect" and "Baby Einstein" were born. Books, CDs and videos quickly flooded the market, claiming to make baby smarter, faster. Infants were put in front of the TV, and relationships with significant caregivers were put on hold. As an educator, this whole idea seemed clearly wrongheaded to me. But young parents were susceptible to the promotional bombardment. Who could blame them? Helping your baby be the smartest, the brightest, sounded like the "right" thing to do.

Coinciding with this phenomenon, I became a grandmother for the first time. What was I to do? Well, as any new, responsible grandmother would, I voiced my opinion to anyone who would listen, even though I knew I was traveling this road somewhat alone. Eventually, though, I found experts who shared my view, and now, seven years later, our society is beginning to get it.

We are moving past the "leave no child behind" movement. Parents are starting to leave Einstein in the science books, rather than making him part of their babies' curriculum. Parents need to unite and say no to academics in the crib, on the highchair or potty. Children need their childhood, and they need it now more than ever.

As en educator and grandmother, I believe music is one of the single most important gifts you can give your children. It will affect their entire development, including supporting their emergent literacy. But while reading books, even to your unborn child, is important by itself, it would be a sad omission if singing were not part of parents' daily interaction with their children. Music can provide children with all they need from the onset.

Children are born seemingly pre-wired for music. They enter the world ready and expecting to move. And that is how they learn. Researcher Lori A. Custodero tells us that "rhythmic and melodic dialogue begin in the birthing room.… Music is meaningful to very young children and motivates them to participate physically, emotionally and cognitively."

It would follow, then, as Janet Greene believes, that music teachers are also language-arts teachers. As my own music program evolved, I came to realize that music and movement also teach language, action words and spatial concepts. Many studies have shown that by actively listening to and making music, children are acquiring many early literacy concepts and skills, including phonemic awareness, syllables, rhyme, parts of speech, grammar, vocabulary and spelling.

M is for the Many Things She Gave Us—Mother Goose, That Is . . .

At Bridgewater State College, in Bridgewater, Massachusetts, a study was conducted to assess and expand kindergartners' phonological awareness. Unexpectedly, the college students also discovered the children's lack of exposure to Mother Goose rhymes.

Literally Speaking

- Children with a strong sense of the beat are more likely to read well.
- Music stimulates all the senses, helping children learn to recognize patterns and sequence.
- Early music exposure helps children learn by promoting language, creativity, coordination, social interaction, self-esteem and memory.
- Singing games support children's need to socialize and play, instead of "pre-academic" skills.
- Music helps "wire" the brain, supporting a higher level of thinking.

When I read about this study, I was not all that surprised. Over the years, when conducting workshops, I had often been shocked at how many teachers did not know Mother Goose. When I presented the rhymes, the young attendees yawned, while the older ones asked for more. It seemed that somehow an entire generation had missed out on this basic component of Americana. The family unit has changed, with extended families now living far apart and the front porch or kitchen table no longer setting the stage for grandparents to recite poems and share with little ones.

A very small percentage of the children in the Bridgewater study knew a few rhymes, but except for an occasional child, even they hadn't heard the rhymes from the "expected source—a family member." When they were asked how they knew a particular rhyme, they responded, from Barney, from Dora, from *Blues Clues,* from a tape, from the computer. "I have a book with a button, and it sings 'Humpty Dumpty' to me." When I finished reading this study, my heart was aching. Such a simple moment of love, so easily shared one on one, had been delegated to technology.

J. Glazer suggests that hearing nursery rhymes read at school "provides a link between home and school that fosters a feeling of security." But how can this happen if the children aren't hearing the rhymes at home? How have we stopped setting aside a little time to read to our children, instead putting them in front of the TV or the computer?

In writing about the Bridgewater study, Mary E. Shorey points to not only the "importance of rhymes in phonological awareness development, but also the importance of Mother Goose rhymes in perpetuating our literary heritage." These rhymes link generations together.

Indeed, according to Shorey, Mother Goose rhymes are children's first experience with literature. R. Lukens labels nursery rhymes as a child's "most natural introduction to poetry." Shorey describes these verses as "tightly constructed stories" containing all the literary elements children find in other forms of literature: "Children are also introduced to new vocabulary, figurative language, and nonsense. These all make for interesting activities with language."

Here's an idea for a class project that Shorey's students devised:

- While working with a college buddy, each child was introduced to Mother Goose rhymes, the children reciting the rhymes with their buddies.

- Each child was then given a sheet with a dozen of the rhymes that were recited. The rhymes were discussed, and each child selected a personal favorite.

- Each child's favorite rhyme was cut from the sheet and pasted on a page of the child's "All About Me" book, illustrated by the child.

- A class favorite was then chosen, each child choosing by writing her or his name or initial on a sticky note and coming forward one at a time to indicate their favorite by placing their sticky note on a poster that showed the various titles.

- Each child got a page of the winning rhyme for his or her book, and each child highlighted all the important (rhyming) words, with the help of his or her buddy.

This activity, Shorey points out, helped "the kindergarteners' [develop] rhyme awareness [and] allowed them to identify sounds in words and to look for the letters in words that represent the rhymes."

Shorey further notes a 1980s study that "reported that 3-year-olds who have a great deal of exposure to nursery rhymes and have memorized several verses are more like to have higher levels of phonemic awareness when they enter Kindergarten." Researchers, she tells us, in fact "[contend that] the one of the best indicators of how well children will learn to read is their ability to recite nursery rhymes when they walk in the kindergarten!"

Rhyme on, Mother Goose, rhyme on.

Read More about Language

Apostoli, Andrea. "Music, Sound and Voice in the Prenatal Relationship between Mother and Child: Leading Groups of Pregnant Women according to Music Learning Theory." *AUDEA* 12, no. 3 (2008).

Baney,Cynthia Ensign."Wired for Sound: The Essential Connection between Music and Development." *Early Childhood News* (March–April 1991).

Bayley, Ros. "Music Appreciation: A Universal Language for All Ages." http://www.naeyc.org/ece/1997/asp.

Condon, W., and L. Sandler. "Neonate Movement Is Synchronized with Adult Speech Interactional Participation and Language Acquisition." *Science,* January 11, 1974.

Coulter, Dee Joy. "Music and the Making of the Mind." *Early Childhood Connections: Journal of Music and Movement-Based Learning* 1, no. 1 (1995).

Feierabend, John M. "Music and Movement for Infants and Toddlers, Naturally Wonder-full." *Early Childhood Connections: Journal of Music and Movement-Based Learning* 2, no. 4 (1996).

Gabrieli, John. "Musically Trained Children Process Language Better." *USA Today,* November 17, 2005. http://www.melodyhounds.com/USA_111705.html.

Gardner, Howard. "Do Babies Sing a Universal Song?" In *Readings in Early Childhood Education.* Reston, Va.: MENC, 1992.

Glazer, J. *Literature and the Young Child.* Upper Saddle River, N.J.: Prentice-Hall, 2000.

Greene, Janet "Making Language Connections through Orff Schulwerk." *Orff Echo* (Winter 2006).

Harman, Maryann Y. "Music and Movement: Instrumental in Language Development." Clearwater, Fla., 2005.

Hopper, Marie E. "Rollickin' Rhythm Sticks." *Pass It On: Journal of Children's Music Network* 54 (Autumn 2006)

Lightbrown, Patsy, and Nina Spada. *How Languages Are Learned.* Oxford: Oxford University Press, 1993.

Madaule, Paul. *When Listening Comes Alive: A Guide to Effective Learning and Communication.* Norval, Ont.: Moulin Publishing, 2004.

Miller, Eric. "Verbal Play and Language Acquisition." 2003. http://ccat.sas.upenn.edu/~emiller/Amiga_article.html.

O'Donnell, Ann. "The Interrelationship of Language Development and Attachment." *Infant Crier: Journal of the Michigan Association of Infant Mental Health* (April–June 2006). http://www.mi-aimh.msu.edu.

Read More about Literacy

Bartel, Virginia B. "Merging Literacies: A Case Study." *Childhood Education* (Summer 2005).

Gauthier, Delores R. "Children's Literature in the Music Classroom: Finding the Music Within." *MENC Journal* (January 2005).

Gittings, Susan B., and Bonnie Hurless. "Weaving the Tapestry: A First-Grade Teacher Integrates Teaching and Learning." *Young Children* (March 2008).

Lukens, R. *A Critical Handbook of Children's Literature.* Boston: Pearson Education, 2007.

McIntire, Jean M. "Developing Literacy through Music." *MENC Journal* (August 2007).

National Head Start Child Development Institute: http://www.hsnrc.org.

Shorey, Mary E. "Meeting Mother Goose: An Introduction to Rhyme." *Focus on Pre-K and K* 20, no. 2 (2007).

Travels with Music: http://www.travelswithmusic.org.

West Bloomfield Township Public Library. "Nursery Rhymes, Songs and Fingerplays." http://www.wblib.org.

LISTENING AND HEARING

Listen, do you want to know a secret?
—**John Lennon and Paul McCartney**

I first became interested in the concept of listening many years ago while walking the shore of Lake Michigan. I was creating a new class called "Movement, Magic & Make-Believe." Eight four-year-olds and I would spend two hours a week together exploring music, movement, art, drama and literature.

It was a daunting undertaking. But when I came to the lake, inspiration kicked in. The peace, quiet and harmony helped it all fall into place. As I began to plan the structure of the class and create ideas for movement and drama, a flock of seagulls scoured the beach in search of their supper.

I listened as they sang overhead and watched them hover over the water in suspended silence to seize their catch of the day. In just a short span of time of watching the birds, ideas poured onto my paper. As the waves grew in velocity, I paused to listen to them lapping at the shore. I tuned into the song of the wind whooshing near and far, closed my eyes and simply "put on my listening ears." I was immersed in a seascape of sounds and splendor.

At that point I connected with the concept of focused listening and the role it could play in making music. I came to realize that our visually oriented culture provides few opportunities for young children to listen. I began to observe my students and their families. I researched materials to see what peaked their interest in listening and if, indeed, they were taking the time to listen.

I subsequently began to develop a listening workshop and, in researching the literature, came upon the work of Paul Madaule, the director of the Listening Centre, in Toronto, Canada. I was instantly drawn to Madaule's easily understood definitions and concepts; his approach greatly influenced my own curriculum.

Madaule's work is based on Alfred Tomatis's belief that defective listening can lead to impaired learning. According to Madaule, "ears control balance, body movements and coordination; they permit language; they make us speak eloquently and sing in tune; they even control our eyes when we read and our arm, hand and finger movements when we write….Interconnected with several different levels of the brain, the ears act as a double antenna receiving messages from both the body and the environment…[acting as] a link between the world within and the world without….Listening brings about the harmony both within us and in our relationship with others….When listening doesn't develop, communication is cut off."

Sometimes one of Madaule's clients will remark that they "hear too much." But, Madaule tells us, "hearing too much means not listening enough….This is precisely what happens with many autistic children, those who cover their ears with their hands to block a sound, who seem hurt by some noises and afraid of them." In

Madaule's clinic, he has found that children and adolescents diagnosed with ADD-LD academic performance difficulties, development disorders and autism all have one thing in common: impaired listening. The intervention Madaule uses is a listening-training program that improves and enhances a person's ability to attune the ear, mind and body—to enhance his or her listening ability. Madaule's program uses both recorded music and singing.

When I first read of Madaule's work, I was thrilled to learn that he used music in his interventions. Listening, I realized, is involved in all aspects of music-making, and most of the activities in my program were focused on enhancing listening skills, calling upon children to anticipate, stop and listen—even babies! Even very young children can learn to focus on music through activities that emphasize listening attentively and appreciatively.

And interestingly, the invaluable lessons I have learned through my experiences asking children to listen have helped me occasionally to spot potential problems and tactfully suggest the possibility of evaluation to parents—again reinforcing the notion that a lot more goes on at music time than just music.

When I read Madaule's work, I was particularly struck by what Tomatis calls the "musical ear." "A particular way of hearing," Tomatis believed, is "associated with an active involvement with music." And further, "what applied to the role of the ear in singing also applied to talking." This really struck a chord with me. I found this discovery exciting beyond words. What a grand piece of knowledge to share with my colleagues and families: "Everything pointed to the fact that there was indeed an active side to hearing; the ear could be wonderfully flexible in adapting to a wide range of situations."

Madaule hypothesizes that children with language delays or impairments, Down's syndrome, autism and learning disabilities may be suffering from impaired listening, related to "right brain" dominance (where the right ear becoming the leading, listening ear). If you have any related concerns about your child, I would urge you to read Madaule's book; his work presents provocative challenges to our traditional understanding of learning.

Prenatal Hearing

You know, this may sound strange, but music has been a part of me since before birth.
—Boris Bott-Hamilton,
conductor of the Ontario Philharmonic

In researching the importance of music, I found the information on prenatal hearing and listening particularly fascinating. Indeed, Madaule tells us that data show that midway through pregnancy, the infant's eardrum and inner ear have reached adult size. Great musicians have long claimed that their musical interest could be traced to the womb. He quotes Boris Bott-Hamilton, who claims that "all the scores I knew sight unseen were ones that she [his mother, a cellist] had played while she was pregnant with me."

How does this happen? Alfred Tomatis, according to Madaule, theorized that the "unborn child puts her/his head against the mother's spinal column, a column of sound, being directly 'plugged in' to the voice. Towards the end of the pregnancy with the head down against the hip bones of the mother…this body to body connection is [an] initial attempt to listen…[a] first step toward communicating." In fact, Madaule tells us that according to Henry Truby, a six-month-old fetus "already moves his/her body to the rhythm of his mother's speech."

Paul Madaule tells us that:

Listening

- Is at the root of all communication
- Is the ability to tune in to sounds and messages and to tune out at will (and a listening problem is the inability to tune in and out)
- Can also imply hearing too much and not listening enough—as when children cover their ears to block a sound or seem hurt or frightened by some noises

Our ears

- Control balance and body movements
- Contribute to the ability to read and write well
- Control voice production (in connection with the brain)

Communicating

- Begins within ourselves and later leads to harmony with others—and a key to this harmony is the link between the ear and the voice
- Seems to be the primary human need, originating even before the need to be fed, which comes only after birth

Music

- Engages and reinforces the "dialogue" between the ear of the body and the auditory ear. This dialogue is important for the acquisition of motor functions, verticality, space and time awareness, lateral dominance and language.
- Prepares the way for the integration of words, phrases and numbers. One of the purposes of singing nursery rhymes is to attune these two "ears"—bodily and auditory—to make them both listen.
- Should play an essential role in early and preschool life. Harmony between movement and sounds—between the bodily and the auditory ear—is a prerequisite for the acquisition of language and for academic learning in general.
- Brings tranquility. The mother's heartbeat gives the unborn child a sense of security. The heartbeat's repetitive, rhythmic movement is picked up by the vestibular system—the bodily ear of the unborn child. The heartbeat gently rocks the child day and night, bringing a reassuring sense of continuity. This "vestibular perception" may greatly contribute to the imprint of bodily rhythms that pave the way for the future integration of body image, motor functions and language.

Musically speaking, Madaule tells us that:

- Music is energy: there is no better way to start a day than to listen to upbeat music or to sing in the shower. The liveliness of the sounds fills you with vital energy.
- Gregorian chants are "rich in high frequency sounds, which are energizing. They give energy and inner peace to those who chant and those who listen."
- Music fulfills a human need as fundamental as the need to eat.
- The appeal of Mozart's music is universal. Mozart's music is the only music we know that creates a perfect balance between music's charging effect and a sense of calmness and well-being. It relaxes the overly active and the anxious and energizes the tired and the depressed.
- Children with Down's syndrome respond particularly well to the energizing effects of Mozart.
- Rocking, rolling and other movements stimulate the vestibular system—the bodily ear.

This brings home for me how truly important it is to talk, read and sing to your unborn baby throughout your pregnancy. Madaule even recommends that a pregnant woman should "synchronize her movements with the sound of her voice"—rocking while reading a story or reciting a poem, dancing while singing.[9]

Take yourself and your children to the woods, the beach, a park—anywhere outdoors, without the sounds of traffic or the city—and "put on your listening ears." In the stillness, there is much going on and much to be heard. These simple listening experiences will enrich your life and help you find some peace and quiet in this noisy world.

Read More about Listening and Sound

Apostoli, Andrea. "Music, Sound and Voice in the Prenatal Relationship between Mother and Child: Leading Groups of Pregnant Women according to Music Learning Theory." *AUDEA* 12, no. 3 (2008).

Madaule, Paul. *When Listening Comes Alive: A Guide to Effective Learning and Communication.* Norval, Ont.: Moulin Publishing, 1994.

Sims, Wendy L. "Learning to Listen—Listening to Learn." *Perspectives* (Winter 2006).

Thomas, Verny. *The Secret Life of the Unborn Child.* New York: Dell Publishing Company, 1981.

---

[9] A very special thanks to Paul Madaule of the Listening Centre for his permission to reprint passages from his wonderful book *When Listening Comes Alive.*

7

Rock-a-Bye Baby

A, you're adorable,
B, you're so beautiful,
C, you're a cutie full of charms.
D, you're a darling,
and E, you're exciting and
F, you're a feather in my arms....
—Buddy Kaye, Fred Wise, and Sidney Lippman

Often I'm asked, "Just what *do* you do with those babies?" And I always respond with the same answer: "Plenty!" And research data supports the importance of musical play for infants—not only for fun but often as therapy for premature babies and infants in the ICU. I may not be a degreed therapist, but as a music educator and grandmother, I have seen firsthand how powerful music really is, how it impacts both infants and caregivers in many ways.

Infants come into the world with an innate receptivity to music and movement. Research in fact suggests that music positively affects all areas of development, nourishes the brain and creates opportunities for social-emotional competence. Since hearing is the second sense to develop in utero, the baby dance practically begins at conception. Immersed in sounds and rhythms, babies are seemingly pre-wired for music. They enter the world ready and expecting to move.

But the current focus on academics may leave the crucial role of social-emotional development behind, and it is difficult for children to develop cognitively if this emotional component is not stable. Music can be at the core of the social connections formed between children and their caregiver. Music, indeed, can be the caregiver's best friend, an indispensable tool that can instantly transform a cranky environment into one of harmony and even joy.

Parents may be faced with a situation that seems overwhelming. Perhaps a parent is young or inexperienced, isolated, overwhelmed, unprepared, scared, lacking in resources or sleep-deprived. But a simple song can calm the uncertainty of transition for mom or dad. Sometimes new parents are not inclined to put their baby at the center of their lives, or they may lack the skills to be confident and effective music makers. But even the simplest music can be very powerful, indirectly placing baby at center stage. A song might be the only tool that is always available to help in a frustrating situation.

Music and movement can also greatly enhance a baby's sense of trust, thus laying the foundation for cognitive and social-emotional well-being. Such early musical experiences will affect families for years to come—truly a gift that keeps on giving. We know that music can have a huge impact on families and parenting. The significant caregiver can in fact be thought of as a child's first favorite toy. "The human voice," according to Sandra Trehub, "[is] unmatched for its intimacy vs. playing recorded music."

And babies themselves are extremely capable singers. Learn the "bahs" and "bums" from the voice-exploration segments detailed below, or make up your own. And don't forget to pause, waiting for baby to answer. Echo your baby's sounds, always, again, waiting for a response. Create conversations.

And the power of music reaches beyond families. I often wonder what the baby who enters daycare at six weeks is thinking and feeling. Confused? Scared? Where is that familiar voice and smell? How lucky for the daycare provider who can effectively put that precious little one at ease just by singing a simple tune.

Remember that babies get their first view of the world from us, learning about trust, safety and love. Caring for an infant is the most important job I know of, and music can be the caregiver's best friend.

Musical activities

- Enhance the parent-child bond through touching and rocking

- Nurture the caregiver as well as the baby, strengthening confidence and self-esteem

- Affect the total development of the child

- Nourish the brain

- Establish a strong language-movement connection

- Create a foundation for listening, learning and literacy

- Provide opportunities for grounding, body awareness, problem solving, balance and coordination

- Can transform a cranky mood instantly into a joyous one

Music can make even everyday tasks into special, positive experiences. Whether it's changing time, feeding time, naptime or time to bundle your child into the dreaded snowsuit, adding a chant or song can turn a task into a treat.[10] Doing so will calm not only the baby but also the caregiver: babies easily pick up on adults' frustration, and this simple technique can make a huge difference in how everybody feels in the end.

A single melody can be used for various situations. To illustrate, the teasing melody "na-na-na-na-na" can easily be put to more positive use:

You are so cranky, I'm cranky too.
We're both so cranky, now what should we do?
I have an answer, let's sing a song.
Then we won't be cranky for too very long.

Somebody's tired. I wonder who?
Somebody's tired. (Name), must be you.

Here comes your diaper. It's fun to do.
First before I change you, I will kiss you.

Hello to (name), hello to you.
Hello to you. How do you do?

Going to the park (to the mall, for a walk).
Going to the park (to the mall, for a walk).
Grandma and (name) are going to the park.

I love you, I love you.
(Name, name), I love you.

---

[10] See chapter 10 for more specific infant activities.

Read More about Babies

- Beaubien, Brigid. "Elizabeth Cady Stanton's Advice to Parents." *Infants and Toddlers* (Spring 2007).

- Feierabend, J. M. "Music and Movement for Infants and Toddlers, Naturally Wonder-full." *Early Childhood Connections: Journal of Music and Movement-Based Learning* 2, no. 4 (1996).

- Hunter, Tom. "Some Thoughts about Sitting Still." *Young Children* (May 2000).

- "The Musical Lives of Babies and Families." *Zero to Three: Bi-Monthly Journal* (September 2002).

- Olson, Carole, and Cheryl Schneider. "Rock-a-Bye Baby Reader." Third Weeks Books. http://thebabyreader@yahoo.com.

- "Prelude to a Musical Life: Prenatal Music Experiences." *Music Educators Journal* 71, no. 7 (1985).

- Rofrano, Frances. "Make Space for Infant Spirituality." *ACEI Focus on Infants and Toddlers* (Spring 2008).

- Shore, Rebecca. *Baby Teacher: Nurturing Neural Networks from Birth to Age Five.* Lanham, Md.: Rowman and Littlefield, 2002.

- Szamrreta. Joanne. "Peekaboo Power: To Ease Separation and Build Relationships." *Young Children* (January 2003).

- Trehub, Sandra E. "The World of Infants: A World of Music." *Early Childhood Connections: Journal of Music and Movement-Based Learning* 2, no. 4 (1996).

Online Resources

- Centers for Disease Control and Prevention. "Folic Acid." http://www.cdc.gov/ncbddd/folicacid.

- Harvey Karp: http://www.thehappiestbaby.com.

- William Sears (several books and support resources): http://www.askdr.=sears.com.

- Zero to Three: http://www.zerotothree.org.

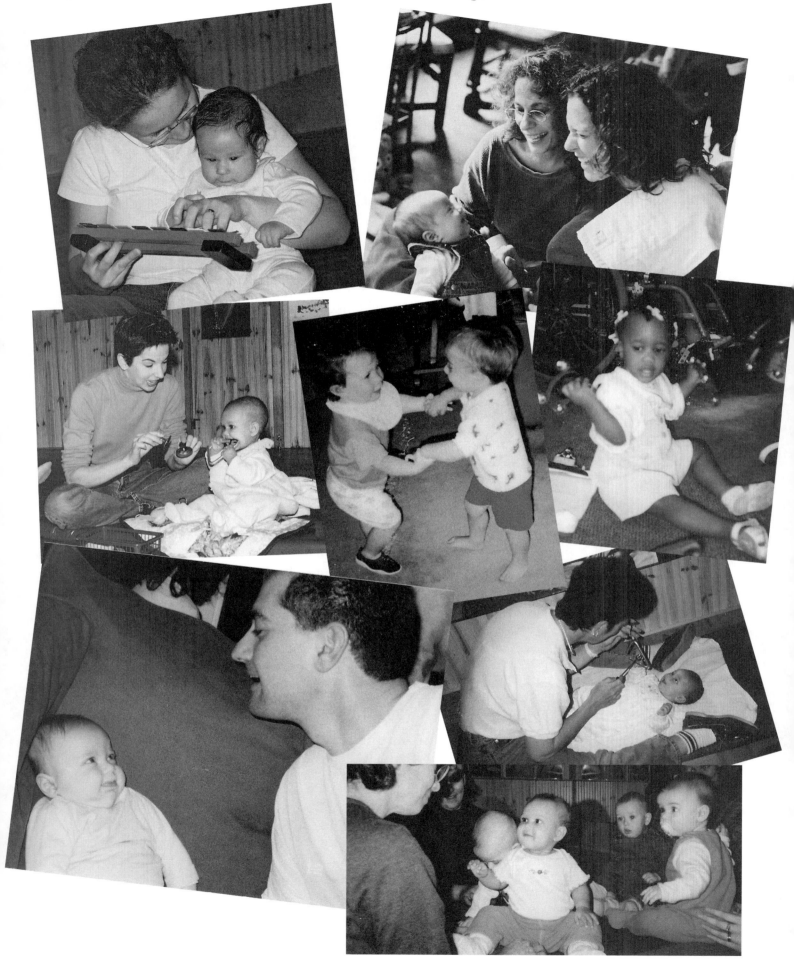

Part 2
THE ACTIVITIES
Too Much Fun (and Educational)
for Everyone

8

LET'S START AT THE VERY BEGINNING . . .

...a very good place to start.
When you read you begin with A-B-C,
When you sing you begin with do-re-mi, do-re-mi.
The first three notes just happen to be do-re-m, do-re-mi.
—**Rodgers and Hammerstein**

Adults need to give children space to approach music and movement in their own manner and on their time frame. Remember, little ones have individual learning styles too. They might:

- Actively participate
- Observe
- Be slow to warm up
- Choose to sit, stand or wander
- Explore materials in their own way, rather than the "correct" way

You are your child's first teacher. Remember:

- Watching is always a valid form of participating.
- No matter how innocent it may seem, helping a child will often interrupt his or her process.
- Children need time to just be.
- Saying "good job" may make children more dependent than saying "you did it" or "how did you do that"—or saying nothing at all (Alfie Kohn).

The Group Setting

Before You Get Started

Since the structure of music programs tends to be directed by adults, be sure to provide many opportunities for child-initiated extensions of activities. Add suggestions for creative movement whenever possible. Ask the children questions to engage them: What else can we do? How else can we move? Let them add their ideas and take turns being the leader. Allow time for free exploration of instrumental music, ribbons, scarves and small percussion instruments. When young children create vocal sounds, imitate them: answer and create conversations.

Music enriches children's lives and taps into their creative energy, and we need to allow them the freedom to explore and be spontaneous.

Don't Be Afraid

Making music with young children, especially involving movement, might seem scary at first. Many parents and educators, regardless of their education or expertise, fear the possibility of losing control of the group. Here are some tips for maintaining control:

- Honor individual learning styles.
- Use age-appropriate materials.
- Keep the pace moving.
- Give children time to explore and add their ideas.
- Keep directions to a minimum by modeling and singing, rather than speaking.
- Stop before they tire.

Often, too, adults are concerned about doing music because they don't play an instrument. But children actually attend better when voice is not accompanied. Don't be afraid to sing. You can, and you must! Your enthusiasm and joy will become your voice. Sandra Trehub, of the University of Toronto, asserts that live singing, as compared to recorded music, is "unmatched for its intimacy and expressiveness even when it fails to meet conventional standards of excellence."

Don't Fence Me In

We know that young children learn by moving, touching, seeing, listening, tasting. They may learn equally through all their senses, but they learn mainly by absorbing and moving. The use of carpet squares and rules like "sit on your bottoms" are not appropriate during music time. Such restrictions deny young children their natural instinct to move and might actually stifle their creative energy. They may even be detrimental to children's sense of self and affect their emotional and aesthetic development.

Remember: by respecting individual learning styles, we are supporting children's growth and development. Some need to stand, wander or keep their distance from the group. "Just" listening should always be an option: it is an important part of learning. Children need to listen to music before they can make it. Watching, too, is a valid form of participation. Allow time for

silence between activities. Often, this is when learning happens.

In the classroom, I prefer random seating rather than a formal circle. Some children like to sit close to me. Also, random seating helps children negotiate their own space. When I hear "I can't see," I ask the child to find a place where she or he can see, or I ask the group to help the child find such a place. I learned from Bev Bos that this subtle gesture empowers children.

When working with families, however, I find that a circle works well. The child who is antsy often does well sitting on a lap or against a wall. Talk as little as possible. Sing or model as much as you can.

A Spoonful of Sugar

Music is a must in every childcare setting. Hearing and singing appropriate music on a daily basis is important for the young child, but not just any music will do. Stay away from music that is too loud, too fast, too busy. Traditional rhymes, songs and melodies help to preserve our rich heritage.

Use care when choosing materials. Be aware of stereotyping in songs, finger plays, puppetry and storytelling. Does your Thanksgiving celebration focus on turkey, teepees, feather headbands and face painting? Consider the importance of the foundation you're providing for children. Will your choices make their view narrow and rigid, or broad and varied, helping them to learn acceptance, tolerance and compassion? Think about:

- Gender equality
- All styles of families
- Diverse ethnicity
- Older people
- Nontraditional roles

Enhance books and stories by incorporating movement and art. Look for opportunities to include creative movement whenever possible. If this is your first time working with music in a group setting, don't try to work through the whole format in one sitting. Start with a hello song one day, and add bits and pieces here and there. If you're in the classroom, make music part of your curriculum every day, all day long. It's not just for circle time: try singing a storybook instead of reading it.

Children Can Easily Be Engaged for Thirty Minutes

- Give children time to absorb the music briefly after each activity.
- Keep the pace moving.
- Plan more activities than may be needed.
- Always have alternative plans. When something isn't working, stop and try another day.
- Be open to spontaneity, incorporating children's ideas on the spot, whenever possible.
- End too soon rather than going on too long.

We Gather Together

Rather than celebrating the holidays, consider celebrating the seasons, perhaps inviting families to get together for seasonal potlucks and sing-alongs. Such a simple gesture can really bring people together and build community.

And community—including adults and children—is what this is all about. When I take my family program on the road and meet with new folks, I always have some gentle reminders for adults:

- Have fun.
- Leave expectations at the door, and let the children approach the music in their own manner.
- Focus on the activity, and enjoy this special time with their children.
- Don't be preoccupied with performance.
- Don't interrupt a child's process by telling or showing him or her what to do.
- Use this time as an opportunity to learn new techniques to try at home, especially when chaos breaks loose.

Read More about Early Childhood and Music

Bredekamp, S., and C. Copple, eds. *Developmentally Appropriate Practice in Early Childhood Programs Serving Children from Birth through Age Eight.* Rev. ed. Washington, D.C.: National Association for the Education of Young Children, 1997.

Fox, Donna Brink. "Music Development and the Young Child." *Music Educators Journal* 77, no. 5 (1991).

Loong, Chet-Pang. "Early Childhood Music: Materials and Activities: Criteria and Guidelines for Selecting and Using Materials in Early Childhood Music Lessons." *OAKE-Kodaly Envoy Journal* (Summer 2007).

"Prekindergarten Music Education Standards." In *The School Music Program: A New Vision: The K–12 Standards, PreK Standards, and What They Mean to Music Education.* Reston, Va.: National Association for Music Education, 1994.

Trehub, Sandra E. "The World of Infants: A World of Music." *Early Childhood Connections: Journal of Music and Movement-Based Learning* 2, no. 4 (1996).

LET'S GET STARTED

9

One for the money.
Two for the show.
Three to get ready
And four to go!

Home Sweet Home

There's no place like home.
—Lyman Frank Baum

This chapter emphasizes methods for a group setting, but all its activities can easily be adapted for a home setting. And that is really the essence of this book. No formal music class available in your community? Invite some families over, and start your own. It's easy. You can use all the steps and activities you'll find here repeatedly, to your children's delight.

With many young children spending more time in daycare than at home, often our time together—what little there may be—is built around rushing out the door, sitting in front of the TV and then hurrying off to bed. What tools music and the arts can be, helping families build relationships that will last forever.

Try a sing-along while preparing dinner instead of putting on the TV. Take time to sing or read before bed. Have art materials always available where children can be messy without worry. Give it a try. See what happens. Such simple steps can change the home environment from chaotic to calm, with little effort or expense. Remember: you are your child's first and most favorite toy. Play it for all it's worth.

The Basic Format and Methods

Throughout your music time, listen for pauses during and between individual songs, including them whenever possible. Pauses help to slow the pace and create silence, which gives children time to hear the music in their heads or repeat it aloud.

It's also helpful to have a basket of stuffed animals (dollies) ready when the children arrive or at music time, allowing each child to pick one. The dollies help take the focus off the child and are a vehicle for independence, finger plays and bouncing.

Hello

Begin and end every music session with a hello/goodbye song, addressing each child by name.

Centering

While sitting with legs crossed (not "Indian-style"—perhaps "like a pretzel"), rock from side to side, pushing off the floor with your hands, while singing a simple "lah-dah-dah-dah" melody. This helps participants to calm, center and find their balance, while nourishing the brain. It also helps to establish a routine, telling children that it is the beginning of music time.

Basic Format

- Hello
- Centering
- Finger Plays
- Tickles
- Hello Dollies: Ready to Bounce
- Bounces and Chants
- Goodbye Dollies: Endings
- Simple Songs and Melodies
- Standing Up and Moving
- Follow the Leader
- Circles/Sit Down
- Listening
- Rock and Row
- Instrument Activity
- Voice Exploration
- Ribbons and Scarves
- Seasonal Songs
- Lullaby
- Finger Plays
- Centering
- Goodbye: The Goodbye Whisper
- Tickles

Finger Plays

When presenting a new finger play, pause after each phrase. This gives children time to hear the words silently or repeat them out loud. Repeat each finger play twice, changing hands.

With infants, look into their eyes, and let them watch your mouth and make eye contact. Do the motions on their hands, feet or tummies. As children get older, they can do motions on their caregiver or on their stuffed animals (dollies).

Tickles

Tickles can be done on infants' palms, feet or tummies. Older children can do them on a dolly, a grown-up or each other. Repeat each tickle twice.

Hello Dollies: Ready to Bounce

Before the bouncing begins, we sing hello to our dollies, which gives the children a chance to sing back. After singing "We'll sing and we will play," I bounce my own dolly silently four times and then say, "Let's bounce, bounce, here we go." Repeat each chant and bounce twice.

Bounces and Chants

Prepare to Bounce

To get ready for bounces, adults hold infants on their laps, supporting their backs, positioned so that they can look into the babies' eyes and the babies can see their mouths. Adults gently bounce or tap older babies on their legs or feet. Toddlers and older children are given a dolly to bounce. I don't recommend moving children's hands for them once they are five or six months old, unless there is a special physical need, as this can inhibit self-exploration. If children want to hold on to their adult's thumbs or arms, that's fine, because then they have the freedom to let go. As babies get older, caregivers can also put their palms up for babies to tap on. Watching and listening is always okay.

Leg Bounces

Leg bounces (demonstrated on the DVD) are especially fun and great for your thighs. With babies, wait until their backs are strong enough and they can hold their heads up on their own. Older children can do these leg bounces with their dollies.

My five-year-old granddaughter still insists that I do leg bounces with her. They're quite a workout, but great fun. Lie on your back, with your knees up toward your chest and your feet off the ground. Your baby's tummy should be on the bottom of your legs, your hands under your baby's arms. Gently bounce your legs during the rhyme.

To end, gently lift your legs at a forty-five-degree angle so that your baby can easily slide down to your chest for a great big hug. Never let go of your baby's arms.

Goodbye Dollies: Endings

Singing goodbye to your dollies, lift them up and down on the first set of "bums" and drop them into the basket at the end of the second set of "bums." This is an ending that I always use to put materials away. It works like a charm, although sometimes there are children who are not ready to relinquish their dolly or materials just yet. That's okay.

To signal the end of an activity without materials, lift your arms or your baby up and bend down on the final "bum" in the same manner.

Simple Songs and Melodies

Without dollies, sing a simple song or nursery rhyme. I usually also include a melody-song without words. I first learned about this method from Edwin Gordon, who developed "music learning theory." The idea is that words may make it difficult for young children to focus on the music. To make music, children need to audiate—to hear the music in their heads when it is no longer physically present. Adding such simple melodies and chants works wonders. I find that even the youngest children respond almost immediately to wordless melodies. In fact, I encourage parents and other caregivers to include them spontaneously throughout the day. You might feel silly at first, but practice them in a closet and come out when you're ready. The results are impressive. Melodies give children opportunities to really focus on listening, to anticipate tempo changes and to experience continuous flow.

Standing Up and Moving

Now it's time to start moving. Again, remember that some children prefer to watch rather than to move with the group—they'll join in when they're ready: watching is always okay. Trying to coerce a child to participate is usually not a good idea. I tell the adults that once children are over two years old, it's in their best interest to sit with them if they still want to be held, rather than lug them around during movement. I know adults often think it's better to carry their children around than to sit and watch, but I find this can lead to an unnecessary power struggle, often even prolonging children's dependence. The child will be ready to join in within only a week or two or after several. Children know when they're ready, and respecting their wishes in this regard will, again, help them become more confident and independent.

During movement, everyone does not have to move in the same direction around the room. A little organized chaos, in fact, helps children to be more aware of their space and to negotiate it.

Limit the use of recordings that give directions to children.

Hold babies so that they're facing the group. Tap-bounce-walk on fast parts, and sway-rock on slow parts.

Movement

Movement can include attention to beat, continuous flow, moving around the room, group circles and the self-exploration of creative ideas. For songs that change tempos or have two distinctive sections, you might tap or bounce your legs for one section/tempo and rock from side to side or move about the room for the other. This is also a good time to explore concepts: high/low, fast/slow, heavy/light, stop/freeze/make a shape. Provide opportunities for imagery and creative movement with older children whenever possible.

Too, educators should remember that movement in the classroom should occur throughout the day, not just at music time.

Musical Selections

Be selective with the recorded music you choose: focus on high-quality classical, jazz, folk or something from your or the children's ethnic backgrounds. Instrumental music, without words, is best. Most public libraries have music you can borrow, and High/Scope Foundation provides a wealth of diverse musical selections. Music should not be too loud, too fast or too slow. Two beats per second for about two minutes is recommended.

Follow the Leader

"Get ready to follow the leader. Can you do what I do?" This activity can be done without props or holding small paper plates, one in each hand. Give children time to explore various ways to move, and ask them for ideas. Place hands or plates where you intend to begin before the music starts. Tap body parts using two hands or plates. Continue the same motion long enough for children to follow, but not so long as to become monotonous (often two phrases works well). Listen for changes in the music to change your motion. Many children choose to watch, and again, that's okay: it's the listening that's important. Start out by being the leader yourself, but incorporate children's ideas and let older children be the leaders too.

Following are some suggested motions that even toddlers can do. Remember to use both hands . . .

- While standing, tap your head/shoulders/tummy/legs, etc., each for a phrase or two.

- With your arms straight overhead, swing them from side to side like wipers.

- Hold your arms straight out in front of you and bounce your hands.

- Twisting from the waist, swing your arms in front of and behind you.

- With your arms down at your sides, swing them forward and back.

- With your hands on your hips, shake your hips from side to side.

- Turn in a circle clockwise and counterclockwise.

- While tapping your legs, tap down to your knees.

- On your hands and knees, rock back and forth.

- Repeat the standing motions that can be done sitting.

- Tap on the floor.

- With plates, it's fun, when the music is over, to skate on them, fan yourselves off, wave them goodbye, put the plates on your heads and drop them into the container with a
  Bum
      Bum
          BUM

Circles/Sit Down

In my class, we always join in a circle before sitting down. Circles can be hard for children, but they provide a sense of community, so they're worth the time. Young children tend to follow their toes into the center of the circle instead of going around. If you can convince them not to hold hands, however, they may have more success. It's easiest for them to walk alone or to hold a caregiver's hand, moving in the direction of the circle. *But:* many children love holding hands, and this is more important than getting it right. With new walkers or toddlers, try standing behind them, holding both their hands. Babies should be held so that they face the inside of the circle.

Try a simple folk dance. Everyone loves "Bim-Bam," and we do it in every one of my classes. Use music you especially like, preferably without words. Pick childhood favorites that reflect your family's heritage, or have other families bring in music from their own backgrounds. One simple approach is to walk in one direction with a quick step (double time), come in and out of the center twice with a slower step (half time), and then repeat.

Again, when babies are present for the folk dance, hold them around their tummies so they can see the other children. Around eighteen months (or sometimes younger), toddlers are often ready to try it on their own. If older children insist on being held, try being the audience and sit out with them until they're ready to join in. This can prevent a lot of power struggles and aching backs.

Listening

"Put on your listening ears. Give those lips a zip-zip-zip!" Sound effects are an excellent source for listening and available in your local library. (The "Sing With Me" CDs also include listening segments.)

To perform a simple focused listening activity, record two similar or opposite sound effects on blank cassettes. Place a portable tape player on the floor, in the middle of the group; this helps get children's interest, and they wait eagerly to hear the first sound. I purposely leave several seconds of silence at the beginning to peak their interest. The adult leading the activity needs to be animated, leaning his or her head and cupping each ear as if getting ready to listen. Throughout the segment, make facial gestures and eye contact to help keep children engaged.

If other grown-ups are present, I remind the children not to let their adults talk to them, so they can focus. Children cannot listen if they are interacting with their caregiver. If children want to talk or engage their caregiver, I suggest that the adult put a finger to their lips or cup an ear to indicate that this is time for listening. This re-

ally works. Anyone who says toddlers cannot listen will change their mind after witnessing this activity. Even the babies are listening! When the sounds have stopped, the children can imitate or talk about them.

Try to provide opportunities every day for focused listening. Children can use their hands, arms and bodies to help differentiate elements such as high/low, loud/quiet, tempo changes, fast/slow and repeated patterns of music and instruments. Before a listening activity is presented in its entirety, play the music through several times, asking the children to put a finger on their nose when they hear the section they are listening for. With older children, music and scarves can be added to extend the activity.

Rock and Row

This partner activity helps children experience beat and flow while gently rocking back and forth.

Until infants are holding their heads up on their own, you should place their back on the thighs of your bent legs, with your hands supporting them. Once they're holding their heads up, sit them so that they face you on your lap, holding them under the arms, and lift your knees up and down to the beat. Generally, older children will sit on an adult's lap or on the floor, holding hands, and together child and adult will gently pull hands back and forth to the beat. Older babies and toddlers might like to lay their whole bodies face down on your legs.

Other options include:

- Two children, or one adult and one child, sitting face to face, legs outstretched, holding hands

- A child standing behind an adult with her or his hands on the adult's shoulders, pushing back and forth

- A younger child on an adult's lap, both facing

in the same direction, with the child holding the adult's thumbs, while the adult partners with a second child. This can also be done with a third child standing behind the adult with her or his hands on the adult's shoulders, pushing back and forth or off the floor.

Instrument Activity

I try to incorporate one instrument activity in every class or circle time throughout the day, using drums, sticks, bells, shakers, tambourines, tone blocks or bean bags. I don't like to do too many structured instrument activities, as they can be distracting. Also, since it's important for children to explore and use instruments in their own way, I like to provide lots of time for individual exploration. In the classroom, some instruments can be kept in a listening center. More structured activities can help children learn to experience the beat, as well as anticipate tempo changes. I always have one of the same instrument available

---

Other Forms of Rock and Row

- Stretchies—dynabands, or stretchy material sewn or tied at the ends to form a circle—can be pulled back and forth.

- Holding a stretchy, adult and child can sit facing in the same direction, the adult's legs outstretched and the band over the adult's toes, both pulling together.

- Several children and adults can stand around the outside of a hula hoop, holding it with both hands, gently bouncing to the beat of a song. When the activity is over, lift the hoop high and low and put it on the floor. Children can jump or crawl in, out, over the hoop. Ask, "How else can you get in and out of the hoop?"

- A group can hold hands in a circle, swinging their arms back and forth to the beat of a song or rhyme. Arms may be going every which way, but it doesn't matter.

---

for each child: young children cannot be expected to wait their turn much before kindergarten/first grade.

There are many resources for homemade instruments, and children can always tap on the floor or on an open palm with a fist instead of using an instrument. Before implementing instruments, you may want to use just your hands to imitate the instrument's motion while you sing the song. Begin by establishing the beat: I tap four times and then say, "Let's tap—tap, here we go." Repeat each song, chant or melody three times, holding instruments up to indicate the end of the song, before starting over. Of course, there should always be an open jam or parade allowing children to choose their own instruments.

Keeping the Beat

Phyllis Weikart, of the High/Scope Educational Research Foundation, emphasizes the importance of a steady beat, stressing that awareness of the beat can help children be better readers and more successful at math. Awareness of the beat can also contribute to children's ability to concentrate, to get along in a group and to understand space and direction.[11]

Children love opportunities to be the leader while the rest follow their beat. They can tap on a drum or some other instrument or on their legs or with one fist on top of the other. "One potato, two potato" is a great chant for this activity; so are many nursery rhymes.

Please remember that children need to feel their own beat before they can follow the steady beat of a group. Many will have a very fast beat: that's okay. Just follow them, as fast or as slow as they go. Even in a group, when I do this activity I focus my attention directly on the child as I keep her or his beat, modeling a steady beat on body parts, in the air or on the floor.

---

[11] For further information on the power of the beat and Phyllis Weikart's work, see http://www.nfbnet.org/pipermail/blindkid/2004-July/000680.html, and http://www.highscope.org.

Voice Exploration

It's great fun for children to explore their own voices by imitating the sounds you make or creating their own for you to echo back. It's also great for their musical development. Here are some ideas:

- Sing "Itsy-Bitsy Spider" and add sound effects, or sing in a low monster, high mousey or whisper voice or no voice at all.

- Sing up and down the scale using animal sounds.

- Make up rhythmic and tonal patterns, chanting "bahs" or singing "bums" for children to echo back with pretend echo puppets (fingers hidden behind their backs). Pause. Give children time to echo back. Use a pretend microphone for solo echoes.

- A pretend slide whistle is a great way to help children use their head (high) voice: Pass out pretend whistles, ask children what color their whistles are and whether they're working. Ask them to open their whistles all the way up to echo back your sound: "First, my turn." Give them time to echo back your whistle sound with their voices, and then let them make sounds with their voices for everyone to echo. Be sure to tell them to take their pretend whistles home.

- If children spontaneously make up their own sounds or patterns, respond whenever possible and echo back to them.

- Make up conversations using "bahs" and "bums" and exaggerated motions.

Ribbons and Scarves

Each of my classes includes a segment of recorded instrumental music for dancing with ribbons, scarves or crepe-paper streamers. Streamers should not be too long—about eighteen inches—and they can be hand-held or on wooden dowels or shower-curtain rings. With a group, try to make all the streamers the same color.

This activity is always a favorite in my classes. Most children, no matter how reluctant to actively participate, cannot resist a ribbon or scarf. Ribbons help the children by taking the focus off of themselves, helping them to move more freely and progress into creative movement. I always provide one ribbon or scarf for each hand: we want bilateral movement, crossing the midline.

Be sure to give children time to explore with their ribbons or scarves before and/or after the music. If they have absolutely no ideas, model some: sweep the floor way down low or up high, make big circles, dance the ribbon on body parts, twist it with your body.

Before the music begins, the class should put on listening ears and "give our lips a zip-zip-zip," so we can listen to the music. Once the music starts, there should be no talking. This includes parents and teachers. If we can't listen, how can we expect the children to?

Each musical selection should be about two minutes long. (It's helpful to prerecord your selection on an individual ten-minute blank cassette.) If the children are simply standing in one place, suggest about halfway through that they take their ribbons for a walk to get them moving about.

This is a total freedom-of-choice movement activity, as long as the children don't dance their streamers on another person. There is no follow the leader, except at the end. When the music is over, if individual children want to show what they did, the group imitates their movements. At the end, ask the children what else we can do with our scarves. Toss them up high, let them float down, catch them on body parts, keep them in the air, blow on them, make them teeney-teeney or put them on heads to drop into their container with a

Bum

    Bum

        Bum

Continuous Flow

Edwin Gordon's music learning theory teaches us that steady beat is not enough. Indeed, it often isn't recommended as part of the birth–age five curriculum. A child might keep a steady beat, but if it isn't felt deep inside, it might not sound too good. Or in other words, as Gordon says, the music needs to flow. You can provide opportunities for continuous flow by having the children make soup, stirring and using exaggerated movements of the arms, legs, heads and hips, while singing melodies or listening to music. The children should be flowing, comfortable with moving their bodies.

Seasonal Songs

Each of my classes includes two or three seasonal songs at the end. Not all children celebrate the same holidays, but the seasons can enrich any environment, while providing lots of learning opportunities. (See chapter 13 for suggestions for specific activities.)

Lullaby

Lullabies are an important element of early childhood, not just for the babies. Rocking from side to side and back and forth nurtures brain development. Older children might want to be rocked by an adult, or they can rock their pretend babies. Try to sing the lullaby rather than depending on a recording of one.

Finger Plays

Repeat as at the beginning of the class.

Centering

Repeat as at the beginning of the class, giving the children an opportunity to center their bodies again.

Goodbye: The Goodbye Whisper

Sing goodbye to each child by name. Then, while playing a recorded version of the lullaby you just sang, give each child a goodbye whisper from a small finger puppet. I always ask new children if they want a whisper. Some don't want it in their ear, but they may want a whisper on their foot or just a touch. If they don't want a whisper, I say, "Maybe next time." The whisper is a nice way to bring closure. It's also the one time in class that everyone has to wait their turn, and amazingly, no matter how large the group, they all do.

It's Not The End

Toddlers are very capable singers and great observers, taking everything in. They love to take the music home and sing and dance with their dollies.

Threes Please, but Eight Is Enough

The age range from three to eight is quite varied, but most traditional songs, simple or complex, can be adapted for young and old. The basic format outlined here provides a good foundation, but you might omit finger plays, tickles, dollies and lullabies for the kindergarteners through second-graders.

10

What to Do with Those Babies?

Jiggle, jiggle, jiggle, jiggle,
Tickle, tickle, tickle, tickle,
Little sack of sugar, I could eat you up.
Hey, hey, hey, my little honey bunny,
Ho, ho, ho, my little turtle dove.
Hee, hee, hee, my little sweetie, sweetie,
Oh, sweetie, sweetie, I could eat you up.
—Woody Guthrie

The World of Infancy

Leaving the warmth, comfort, rhythms and sounds of the womb, babies begin the new journey. They may sleep most of the first few months, as they adapt to their new environment. If they're lucky, they will be close to their mother—nursed, massaged, caressed and sung to. Paul Madaule, of the Listening Centre, reminds us of "the importance of sensory and motor stimulation for the general well-being and development of an infant."

Madaule goes on to say that "touching and turning your baby add to the sensory stimulation that feeds the brain and helps in the growth of mind and body....Talking and singing to the infant while holding him/her, allows a body-to-body transmissions of the sound." Hold your baby close whenever possible, in your arms or in a sling, instead of transporting him or her in a carrier or a car seat. Kiss babies, hug them, hold them close.

If you're working in a group setting, link up with high school or college students—boys and girls—for one-on-one interaction at music time. Whenever possible, infants should be in their own small group, each with a significant other. The atmosphere should be safe, quiet, calm and gentle, with time after class for sharing and exchanging. This will have the added bonus of giving the students an experience that might impact their parenting skills.

Remember, too, that researchers from Boston University found that infants' body movements "were synchronized with the language sounds they heard." Edwin Gordon tells us, "the highest level of musical aptitude occurs immediately after birth."

So sing, sing, sing to your baby. Recite nursery rhymes and poetry while rocking, so body and ear can work together. And don't forget that the changing table is a great place for rhymes and massage. Your baby's memory and oral and written language will all benefit from the attention.

Rock-Dance-Sway to Mozart

During the first few months of your baby's life, hold him or her and rock-dance-sway to the gentle beat of instrumental music. Try not to be in a noisy room or talking to others, so you and the baby can really hear the music. If possible, do this every day, and see how calming it can be. Hum cheek to cheek. As babies get older, make up simple circle dances, holding them around their tummies so that they can see the other babies if you're in a group. If you're not in a group, do your dance in front of a mirror.

Around eighteen months (sometimes earlier), little ones are often ready to try a circle dance on their own, the caregiver standing behind the child and holding both hands to help him or her navigate.

Some Suggestions: Music for Babies

- Leroy Anderson, "Belle of the Ball"
- Mozart, "Eine kleine Nachtmusik" ("A Little Night Music")
- Mozart, Clarinet Concerto, K.622, Clarinet Quintet, K.581
- Pachelbel, "Canon in D Major"
- Saint-Saens, "Aquarium," "Carnival of the Animals"
- Strauss, "Vienna Waltz," "Blue Danube Waltz"
- Tchaikovsky, "The Nutcracker Suite," "Sleeping Beauty Waltz"

Use any music you like, but remember that it shouldn't be too fast, too loud or too busy.

A Sampling of Infant Activities

Pat and Tap

Gently pat your baby on the legs or back, and avoid tapping on the head.

Ah-ah, ah-ah baby,
Mama is a lady
Daddy is a gentleman
And you're the little baby.

Rickety, rickety, riding horse,
Over the hills we go.
Rickety, rickety, riding horse,
Giddy-up, giddy-up, whoa . . .

Shoe a little horse.
Shoe a little mare.
But let the little colt
Go bare-bare-bare.

Pitty-patty-polt,
Shoe a little colt.
Here's a nail, there's a nail,
Pitty-patty-polt.

Finger Plays

Touch or massage your baby's fingers or toes, one at a time.

This little cow eats grass.
This little cow eats hay.
This little cow drinks water,
And this cow runs away.
But this little cow does nothing,
But just lies down all day.
We'll chase her, we'll chase her,
We'll chase her awaaaaay . . .

Here are baby's fingers.
Here are baby's toes.
Here is baby's belly button,
Round and round it goes.

Tickles

Gently tickle your baby's palm, leg, foot or tummy.

Round and round the garden
Goes the teddy bear.
One step, two steps,
And tickle under there!

X marks the spot, with a dot and a dot,
And a dash and a dash, and a big question mark.
Tickle up, tickle down, tickle all over town,
With a hug and a squeeze.
No more tickles please!

A little flea went walking to see what she could see.
But all that she could see was (name's) tummy.

Round and round the lighthouse,
Up the spiral stairs.
One step, two steps,
And tickle under there!

Massage and Stretch

Gently rub your baby's tummy, back, arms and legs. If possible, join an infant-massage class, which will help with digestion and sleep.

Leg over leg as the dog went to Dover,
When she came to a wall (pause), jump—she
went over.

Up and down, up and down, up and down,
and all around.
Out and in, out and in, out and in, and
round again.

Wash the dishes, wash the dishes.
Ring the bell for tea.
Three good wishes, three good kisses,
I will give to thee.
One kiss, two kisses, threeeee . . .

One leg, two legs, hot cross buns.
One leg, two legs, isn't this fun?[12]

Melodies

For suggestions for melodies, see chapter 8.

"Bahs" and "Bums" versus Words

Try the following:

- Make up patterns using "bahs" and "bums."
- Substitute "bums" for words in familiar songs.

Leg Bounces

Remember to wait until your baby's back is strong enough and he or she can hold up his or her head. Lie on your back, with your knees up toward your chest and your feet off the ground. Your baby's tummy is on your shins, and your hands are under your baby's arms.

Gently bounce your legs during the rhyme. To end, gently lift your legs at a forty-five-degree angle so that your baby can slide down easily to your chest. Try using a rhyme like "Apple Tree" or "Humpty Dumpty."

Remember to never let go of your baby's arms.

Voice Exploration

Try the following:

- Be expressive, using different vocal sounds.
- Roll your tongue to make sounds, lifting your baby up and down.
- Sing "Itsy-Bitsy Spider" using in different voices—high mousey, low monster or whisper voice, or no voice at all.

Instruments

Whenever you use instruments or other props (such as balls, hoops, scarves or tappers), be sure you have enough for all the children to be engaged.

Before babies are able to sit on their own, place them on their backs to track scarves or triangles and finger cymbals while they listen to music.

---

[12] See Lynn Kleiner's ideas at http://www.musicrhapsody.com.

As they begin to reach out, give them a striker or cymbal, and hold your own instrument still for them to tap.

Babies who are sitting up can shake chicitas/little maracas and bells and tap drums, xylophones, triangles, wood blocks, sand blocks and finger cymbals. They can do this to music or while singing songs and melodies.

Rock and Row

- This partner activity allows babies to experience beat and flow while gently rocking back and forth.

Remember: until your baby is holding his or head up independently, place your baby's back on the thighs of your bent legs, with your hands supporting them. Once your baby is holding his or her head up, sit your baby facing you on your lap, holding under the arms. Pull your knees up and down to the beat.

This is fun with almost any nursery rhyme or with old favorites like "You Are My Sunshine" and "Take Me Out to the Ball Game."

Folk and Circle Dances

If you're alone with your baby, hold him or her in front of a mirror and dance to a folk song, turning in a circle and walking toward and away from the mirror.

In a group setting, hold babies facing the center of the circle and walk around the circle, and then walk toward and away from the circle's center.

Try the following:

- Sing "BINGO" one-on-one: With your baby facing a mirror, sway or turn in a circle for the first part of the song. When you sing "B-I-N-G," sing slowly, taking one step toward mirror for each letter and pausing before you sing "O." Then take sliding steps backward on an elongated "OOOOOOOOO."

- Sing "BINGO" in a group: Hold the babies facing the center of the circle. Walk around the circle for the first part of the song, and step toward the center slowly when you sing "B-I-N-G." Step back for "OOOOOOOOO," as above.

Continuous Flow

Holding your baby under his or her arms when the back is strong enough, stir him or her while singing a melody, and watch legs kick with glee.

Sing and Swing

One of the most beneficial activities to do with children is swinging. Swinging nourishes the vestibular system, which is responsible for balance. Sadly, it seems that in our society children are doing much less swinging. So: whether you have a swing in your yard, on the porch or in the park, swing, swing, swing. And while you're at it, don't forget to sing a rhyme or song.

Here are two singing and swinging suggestions:
How would you like to go up in a swing?
Up in a swing so high.
Oh, that would be the most wonderful thing.
Up in the swing. Up to the sky.
Up in the swing so high.

Swing high, swing low.
Swinging high and swinging low.
Bum, bum, bum, bum, bum, swing high.
Away we go, wheeeeee . . .

Tea for Two and Toddlers Too

Most infant activities are also appropriate and easily adapted for toddlers.

When there is not a one-to-one ratio with toddlers and grown-ups, give toddlers a stuffed animal (dolly) to do activities with.

Remember that circle and story time can be difficult for toddlers. Developmentally, they are often just not ready to sit for long or even short periods of time. Find ways to interject music-making and storytelling throughout their day—while waiting for snack, coming in and going outside, during transitions, in the bathroom, on the changing table. Make up conversations using "bahs" and "bums." Songs and stories about animals are especially interesting at this age.

It doesn't take an expert to know that toddlers are always ready to move. If I'm in a roomful of toddlers and they're just sitting, I get nervous. Much of their learning occurs through movement. Tap paper plates on body parts to music. Use crepe-paper streamers, ribbons and scarves for dancing. When children are ready for more routine, try a more structured, yet informal music session (see chapter 8). Improvise, and be spontaneous! The main thing is to get those little ones moving through space and have fun.

Read More about Infants and Toddlers

Gordon, Edwin. *A Music Learning Theory for Newborns and Young Children.* Chicago: GIA Publications, 1997.

Madaule, Paul. *When Listening Comes Alive: A Guide to Effective Learning and Communication,* Norval, Ont.: Moulin Publishing, 1994.

11

A POTPOURRI OF ACTIVITIES
A LITTLE BIT OF THIS…A LITTLE BIT OF THAT…

With gesture, movement and energy, you can say so much to express your deepest emotions and thoughts. Movement is not corrupted by words and their various definitions. Words require the brain for interpretation, but movement is experienced with the heart.
—Ivan Patrov, of the Royal Ballet of London

Mix things up! Partner and listening activities, seasonal celebrations, creative movement—and children's own suggestions—will keep older kids engaged, more apt to play with Mom, Dad, grandparents, teachers, caregivers and each other, while building a foundation in the arts that will stay with them throughout their lives.

Partner Activities

All join hands and swing your partner!

Some young children are not always comfortable holding hands with other children or adults, yet they should have the opportunity to experience musical play with another person. It may take longer to figure out partner activities, but even toddlers should have a chance to move with a partner from time to time. And of course, if a child chooses not to hold hands, all of these activities can still be done with a partner or solo.

Slow-Fast Melody

Couples hold hands or stand face to face, rocking from side to side on the slow part of a song and jumping in a circle on the fast part.

Hula Hoops

Each couple (or group) holds the outside of the hula hoop and bounces it while singing a song or moving in a circle. The hoop can be raised up high and pushed down low. When the hoop is on the floor, children can jump in and out of it and explore other ways of moving inside and outside.

Stretchies

A child sits on an adult's lap, both with their legs stretched out. A stretchy is around the adult's feet. Both pull together while singing a song and at the end count to three, letting the material go with a BOINNNNG! Two children can do the same activity together, sitting and facing each other, pulling the band back and forth, without stretching it around anyone's feet.

Mirroring

With or without streamers, one partner acts as the leader, and the other copies her or his movements. Younger children can start by sitting on the floor, standing up for bigger movements as they get the hang of it. If children absolutely don't get the idea, then an adult can briefly model this activity.

Large Scarves

Partners hold a large scarf or piece of fabric and move with the music. Partners can take turns being the leader, or both can just move in free form. I prefer slow and lyrical musical selections for this activity.

Echo Puppets

Using fingers as pretend puppets, one partner (the leader, adult or child) makes a tonal pattern, chanting "bahs" or singing "bums." The other partner (the receiver) keeps his or her pretend puppets behind the back until he or she brings them out to echo the patterns.

Take turns being the leader and the receiver. You can also try this activity with real puppets. As children get good at this activity, many conversations will emerge with "bahs" and "bums."

Guided Listening

Put on your listening ears!
Take your ears out for a walk.
If your ears knew how to talk,
I'm so sure that they would say,
"Can we sing a song/take a walk/read a
book/do some art today?"

Listening Activities and Recorded Music

When providing listening activities involving recorded music, it's important to first become extremely familiar with the piece. Practice, practice, practice before using music with children. Young children, even toddlers, can listen to music for two to three minutes when they're actively engaged. Following are some easily learned classical-music listening activities that you can do at home or in the classroom to enhance both listening skills and spirits on a cranky day. The results are impressive.

Verdi, "Anvil Chorus"

A section of hammers pounding repeats throughout. When you hear it, pound your fists or tap the floor. Sway your hands and arms through the rest of the music, perhaps asking the children for ideas.

Handel, "Arrival of the Queen of Sheba"

Before the song begins, talk about "loud and quiet" and "many and few." For "loud and quiet," see if the children can identify how many instruments are playing during the music's quiet section. Have them tap their legs loudly when they hear the loud section and quietly when they hear the quiet section.

For "many and few," have the children march in place when they hear many instruments and freeze when they hear just two. Another time, ask the children to walk around the room when they hear a lot of instruments and stop and put their hands on their heads when they hear just a few. I tell the children to put on their hats of high concentration for this exercise, since the music changes very subtly.

Older children can be divided into two groups, one standing very still, while the other walks around waving scarves to the music. When the music changes to only a few instruments, the walking group freezes. When the music changes back to many instruments, the two groups trade places, the standing group taking the scarves and walking, while the walking group stands still.

Saint-Saens, "Fossils"

The xylophone section in this piece, which weaves in and out, represents fossils (dinosaurs). When it comes, ask the children to take their dinosaur feet for a walk. During the other sections, children can move their arms as the music suggests.

You can cup your hand to your ear to give the signal that the xylophone section is coming.

Haydn, "Symphony #94" (Surprise Symphony)

Before the song begins, explain to the children that patrons attending Haydn's concerts often fell asleep. So in order to wake them up, he wrote this symphony: it is very quiet in the beginning, but every so often there is a grand loud part. Explain to the children that during the quiet part, they will walk or tiptoe around the room to the music, waving scarves or streamers. When the very loud "ka-boom" sound comes, they will stop and throw their scarves up in the air. (As the music is playing, be sure to warn the children when the loud sound is coming, as some get a little scared. I always warn them right before: "Here it comes, get ready.") As the music gets more lyrical, children can wave their scarves and move around freely.

Delibes, "Pizzicati" from "Sylvia" (Tiptoe Dance)

This is a follow-the-leader-type activity. Have the children get their tappers ready, the pointer and middle fingers of one hand tapping on the other open palm.

The music begins very slowly. When the introduction begins, start waving your hands in a small motion, bringing them closer to your thighs. Alternating your hands, tap on your thighs with a two-finger tap on your hand at end of each phrase. The music is very easy to follow. Sway your arms high and low, corresponding with the high and low music.

After one time through, ask the children questions about the music and movement: What did we do first? Why did we change to moving our arms high and low? Why did we go back to tapping on our legs?

The next time, instead of tapping on your legs, tiptoe, and stop for the last two taps on your hand, tapping over your head. Tell the children that they can go anywhere in the room, but they can't bump or make sounds.

Rossini, "William Tell Overture"

Tell the children they will be very busy: they will play their trumpets, bang their drums, ride their horses, look to see who is coming, wave their scarves or streamers and play their violins.

The music is very easy to follow. Sitting down and holding onto the reins, ride your horses, bouncing up and down. Quickly look to see who is coming at the end of the phrase. Wave your scarves during the very fast/loud section, and play violins at the interlude. (Don't worry: the music will guide you.)

Everything repeats, and the song ends with waving scarves. I fall back at the end. Great fun.

Transitions

We're floating down the river,
We're floating down below,
We're floating down the river
To the O-hi-o.
　　　　　　　—Traditional

Transitions can be especially difficult for young children. Often, they're asked to stop what they're doing and move quickly from one activity to another, whether at home or in the classroom. When a transition is necessary, remind children ahead of time of how much time they have before they need to be prepared to move on. Limit transitions as much possible so that children have more time to explore where they are in their play.

When I worked in a toddler room, I had ten children and no aide. When I needed to use the bathroom, all the children had to come with me. I brought ten chairs along, and we all sang throughout my potty time. Again, a simple song came to my rescue, helping make the transition easier and much more fun.

Clean Up
It's time to clean up,
It's time to clean up.
It's time to put our toys away
So we can play another day.
It's time to clean up
(Tune: "Three Blind Mice")

Wash Up

Let's go wash our hands,
Let's go wash our hands,
Let's go wash our hands,
So we can eat (lunch, snack).
Roll up the sleeves of your shirt,
Wash off the germs and the dirt,
Oh, let's go wash our hands.
(Tune: "Let's Go Fly a Kite")

Weather

PLEASE THROW OUT THOSE WEATHER WHEELS!

Children do not learn about the weather from wheels. Instead, try running outside and back quickly, so the children can see and feel the weather. Even in rainy, snowy weather, you can run out, check the weather and run right back in. No one ever got sick in my classroom.

You can also have weather pictures available with Velcro so that children can put them up, even if their picture choice isn't correct.

What is the weather?
What is the weather?
What is the weather outside today?
(say) Is it rainy, is it cold, is it sunny,
is there snoooooowwww?
(sing) What is the weather, the weather today?
(Tune: "Waltzing Matilda")

Standing Up

I never just say, "Okay, boys and girls, let's stand up now." It's much more effective and fun to:

- Use a slide whistle, crouching down low and then moving up and down to the whistle, eventually standing all the way up. Babies in arms can be lifted up and down.

- Sing "bums." Sing up the scale while moving up one note at a time. Do the same using animal sounds: "What animal sounds can we make today?"

Sitting Down

Clap your hands, tap your legs, turn yourselves around.
Clap your hands, tap your legs, jump up from the ground.
Clap your hands, tap your legs, now please sit down.

Touch your head. Touch your toes.
Turn in a circle. Bend down low.
Touch your shoulders. Touch your knees.
Tickle your (grown-up's name's) tummy: tickle-tickle-tickle!
And sit down, please.

Moving from One Place to Another

We're following the leader, the leader, the leader.
We're following the leader, wherever (she/he) may go.
We're following the leader, the leader, the leader.
We're following the leader—we STOP!
And touch our nose/touch our toes/make a pose (imitate the leader's pose).

12

SWINGING ON A STAR!
ACTIVITIES TO INTRODUCE CREATIVE MOVEMENT

Would you like to swing on a star,
Carry moonbeams home in a jar,
And be better off than you are?
—Jimmy Van Heusen and Johnny Burk

Often educators tell me they're a little uncomfortable with creative movement. How should they introduce it? How will they maintain control? Teachers from traditional schools especially often exist in a structured environment, their every minute scheduled, working from a set curriculum, utilizing carpet squares. Often there seems to be little room or time left for creative movement.

But young children don't have to be taught how to move creatively. It comes naturally to them. Often the child who has to be reminded to "sit down" during circle time may be enjoying a moment somewhere else in her or his imagination. We need to nurture this joy in moving, this freedom for creativity, before the confines of society put an end to it.

There are many books written on creative movement, some of which are included in the resource list at the end of this chapter. Here I would like to share some activities that I've found particularly useful. Some are original ideas, some borrowed, and some come directly from children. I always try to look to children for their ideas and go with them whenever possible. Does

it really matter if you don't stick to your plan for the day? You never know where a new idea may lead, and the depth of little ones' thinking may surprise you.

Dancing with ribbons and scarves to recorded music is a great place to start. This is something I do every day. For children who don't move spontaneously (yes, sometimes this happens), this activity can be a precursor to creative movement. Even the most reluctant child seldom refuses ribbons and scarves, which take the focus off the individual. Have one ribbon for each hand whenever possible. Children should use both sides of their bodies, which encourages crossing the midline.

Ribbons can be as simple and inexpensive as crepe paper, although they won't last too long. I start with plain ribbons, all in the same color. I also use ribbons tied to shower curtain rings, ribbons fixed to wood dowels, wands with streamers, pom-poms and scarves. I vary the music, using instrumentals—classical to jazz, big band to Broadway. In the classroom, I ask families to bring in music from their ethnic backgrounds.

This is an activity where you don't need to

worry about losing control of the group, although it does help to establish a few guidelines (e.g., don't touch anyone else with your ribbons). I always begin by reminding everyone to "put on their listening ears and give their lips a zip-zip-zip!" As usual, I really mean this, for adults too! Any talking, and the music stops.

At home, get Grandma, Grandpa or Aunt Cecelia to join in the fun. Bring out music that reflects your family's heritage. Just get moving!

Another great place to start is with books, since they give you a story to help generate ideas. I like to start using books with toddlers as soon as they're able to understand the notion of guided movement. One of my favorites is *The Runaway Bunny*, by Margaret Wise Brown. This story has many ideas for movement, and the built-in control is for the child to run-swim-jump back to me. Chapter 15 lists many other titles that suggest movement.

Get Ready

If the idea of moving as a group is new, take some time to talk about personal space. Children should be able to move without bumping into each other. One approach is to ask children to stand and put their arms out to the side, parallel to the floor. If their arms touch anyone else, they are standing too close. I emphasize that we never touch another person unless we ask first or unless touching is part of the activity. No one is allowed to enter anyone else's personal space.

Another activity to help children identify personal space is called "Bubbles and Elephant Holes." The children pretend to blow up a large bubble and then get inside it. The bubble represents their personal space: they cannot touch anyone else or any object when they are in their bubbles. On the "go" signal, the children begin moving through general space, while staying inside their bubbles. On the "stop" signal, the children stop quickly.

Then, to use all of the general space and avoid collisions, tell the children to fill up the "elephant holes" (large open spaces that might allow an elephant to come in and sit down).

Be careful not to model for children all the time. They should have time to think about how they move. Some may not be comfortable moving for a long time.

Don't require children all to move in the same direction. I let them move anywhere in the room, which helps them learn to negotiate space.

Following are some specific ideas for beginning creative movement:

- Say, "Let's stretch to warm our muscles so they're not cold!" Use windmill arms, reach to the sky, touch toes, hold feet together for butterfly wings, make scissor legs, point toes like pencil points, flex toes like fish hooks, do push-ups with hands on the floor. Ask children, "What do you see up there?" Ask individual children to create a stretch for all to imitate.

- Explore concepts like high/low, quiet/loud, big/small, heavy/light. Tap on a drum for low-loud-small, on its rim for high-quiet-small, as the children walk, jump, etc.

- Explore space with body shapes: "Make a really big shape. Make a round shape, a small shape, a shape with corners. Move your shape. Take it for a walk." Try this with and without instruments. Change the shape at the sound of an instrument.

- Explore high/low with shapes: "Do something very low, do something very high. Make it low, make it high. Make a statue shape low or high. Where is yours, high or low? Tell me what you did." Add high and low voices to your movements.

Get Set

Try the following:

- To the beat of a drum, walking across the floor, alternate moving in straight lines, curvy lines, zig-zagging. If necessary, do the movement with the children, saying what the direction is while you move. This activity can also be extended, with children creating a group mural of straight, curvy and zig-zag lines.

- Explore basic non-locomotor movement. Encourage children to find ways to twirl, bend and stretch, always including their suggestions.

- Explore basic rhythmic and locomotor movement. While walking, running, leaning, sliding, etc., ask children to change direction at the sound of a finger cymbal or bell.

- Have the children get used to moving in a continuous flow, using imagery. Stir soup with different parts of their bodies. Sway in a gentle wind, in a storm, on calm waves, like a blade of grass. Twirl like a top, a snowflake. Bend to the front, to the side, to the back, to the floor, like a rag doll, like a robot, like wheat bending in the wind. Rock in a boat, like a swinging bell, like a rocking chair. Rock together, back to back. Move in silence, with voices, with instruments.

- Say, "Move your body like a ———. Put your body in the shape of a ——— or as if you are a ———." Add voices and chants. Repeat the sounds the children make. Try different sounds for the same walk or movement.

Go

Bubbles

Without music, tell the children to get out their pretend bottles of bubbles: "Let's blow some bubbles, catch a bubble, let it fall, land in your hand. Get inside your bubble, move your bubble all around the room. Paint with your bubble. Move your bubble through a bowl of Jell-O, through peanut butter. Kiss your bubbles with fingers, move them under water." Do the same with music. (Try Saint-Saens," Aquarium" or "Carnival of the Animals.")[13]

Paintbrushes

Tell children to get out their pretend paintbrushes: "Paint high to the sky, low to the ground. Paint the walls, flick paint all over, etc." With music (after listening to it ahead of time), paint the sounds you hear, paint the quiet, paint loud sounds by flicking paint all over. Use different body parts as a paintbrush. Swing and jump. Twirl with your brushes. (Try Haydn, "Surprise Symphony.")

Group Sculpture

Ask one child to make a shape. Ask another to make another shape by touching a specific body part to the first child. Continue until all the children are connected. In a large group, do two or more sculptures. When the sculptures are completed, take a picture with a real or pretend camera. With older children, ask them to slowly change their shape at the sound of a finger cymbal or triangle, but to keep the body contact. Ask them to move to a different place in the sculpture at the sound of a drum and to make a new shape (e.g., by moving from high to low).

Clay

Working in partners or small groups, mold each other into a shape. Give the shape a name, and move it into a dance.

Elephant Walk

Explore time, space, energy and direction using arms and hands like elephant trunks.

Heavy/Light

Take heavy steps: make deep footprints in the sand, make no footprints, walk on hot pavement. Run with strength, pushing the air out of way. Run lightly, making hardly any wind.

---

[13] Thank you to John Feirabend for this activity idea.

Robots and Astronauts

Prerecord two pieces of music that alternate choppy sounds with slow and fluid ones. The music can flow from one style to the other or freeze after each.

Collapse and Rise

Talk about falling without hurting oneself, falling on cushy parts and protecting the body.

Then, using a drum, tap on the rim as children rise and get very tall. With a loud sound on the drum, the children collapse. On the rising sound, explore different ideas: run and touch a wall, go back to your personal space, jump up and down, etc.

The Dance of Small Animals

American Indians often danced about animals. Small animals take small steps, always on the lookout for danger.

Taking small steps all around the room, ask children to let their eyes move all around, perhaps while keeping their bodies low. At a loud drum sound, the children freeze, also freezing their eyes in the direction of the sound.

Swallow the Bounce

Let children listen to music with a strong, bouncy beat. Tell them that there is a bounce in the music and that if they grab it out of the air and swallow it, it will make them bounce too. What can the beat make them do besides jump? Put the bounce in different body parts—one at a time, several at a time. Make the bounce smaller and larger.

Magic Paint

First without and then with music, dip specific body parts into magic paint, and fill the air or the floor with straight lines, curvy lines, zig-zags, dots, spots, large and small shapes, shapes up high and down low. Make the last one in a very small place.

Statues and Dancers

This activity works best for kindergarten through third grade.

First without and then with music, divide the children into two groups: dancers (or "movers" or some other name, if children don't want to be called dancers), who are holding scarves, and statues, who have both feet on the ground and don't move, although their stature can be high, low or middle. Dancers can come close to the statues, but they can't touch them. They can go in-between, around and through the statues. Brainstorm to think of words that imply gracefulness. If some students are reluctant, remind them that football payers take ballet to help improve their coordination, and basketball players work to jump higher. At the sound of finger cymbals, the two groups change places.

Long and Short

To begin, talk about long and short sounds, and identify instruments with long and short sounds.

Then have one child (the leader) pick an instrument and announce, in a singing voice, if it makes a short or long sound. The other children are in the ready position, crouched down. The leader then plays a pattern, and the other children move to the pattern and freeze at the end. The leader "melts" each child by a single tap to the instrument, with the last child now the new leader. The new leader sings, "Here we go," and other children resume the ready position.

Imagery, Poetry, Stories

Incorporate imagery, poetry and stories often, every day, being sure to include the children's own written work. Allow them to move however they see fit to express the words they're hearing. Accompany them musically now and then, but remember that moving in silence is a powerful and positive experience.

Keep clipboards with pencil and paper all over the classroom. Write down the children's stories, and tape-record them.

Goodbye Dance

Let the children move across the floor one by one, allowing them as much time as they need. When they reach the other side of the room, or when they are finished, have them stop and hold their shape.

At home, children can do this activity anytime, throughout the day. It's an inspiring way to go to bed!

Read More about Creative Movement

Burton, Leon H., and Takeo Kudo. *SoundPlay: Understanding Music through Creative Movement.* Reston, Va.: National Association for Music Education, 2000.

Lobo, Yovanka B., and Adam Winsler. "The Effects of a Creative Dance and Movement Program on the Social Competence of Head Start Preschoolers." *Social Development* 15, no. 3 (2006).

Turner, Sandra B. "Caretaking of Children's Souls: Teaching the Deep Song." *Young Children* (January 2000).

SEASONAL CELEBRATIONS

13

To everything, turn, turn, turn,
There is a season, turn, turn, turn.
—Pete Seeger

Not everyone celebrates the same holidays, but we all can celebrate the seasons and the change they bring. When we celebrate the seasons, we invite nature into our lives. In the classroom, invite families for a seasonal potluck and sing-along. At home, invite neighbors or just enjoy the company of your own special family.

Summer

Rhymes

Summer is here. The grass is so green.
Sunshine and flowers, summertime dreams.

Fishies live in the brook, birdies live in the trees,
But a home is the very nicest place for a little child like me.

Activities

- Take a nature walk, listening for sounds.
- Make binoculars or listening tubes out of toilet-tissue holders.
- Go on lots of picnics, join a drum circle.
- Celebrate the solstice.

Songs

Summer songs are a must for road trips: "Good Morning, Mary Sunshine," "Oh, Mr. Sun," "You Are My Sunshine," "Five Little Butterflies," "Take Me Out to the Ballgame," "Daisy Bell: A Bicycle Built for Two."

Movement

- With or without music—but always with scarves!—have a beach party, and build sand castles.
- The children are the sand: they can make shapes out of each other, and the wind comes and blows them away.

Fall

Rhymes

Leaves are falling, gently falling, falling to the ground.
One little leaf, two little leaves, three leaves today—
Four little leaves, five little leaves—blow them all away.

Activities

- Take a walk in the rain, and listen for sounds.
- Jump in puddles, fly kites, make preserves and applesauce.
- Laminate paper leaves, and hang them on shower-curtain rings for dancing.

Songs

Try: "Singing in the Rain," "Come under My Umbrella," "Gray Squirrel," "Apple Tree," "Hop Ol' Squirrel," "The Autumn Leaves."

Movement

- Some movement ideas might find bodies in shape of trees: The leaves are blowing in the air, and a big wind comes and blows them out of the trees. The leaves are fluttering in the air, on the ground; rake them into piles.

- Use scarves or mats for puddles, and walk, jump, etc., to music: "Oh, oh, don't step in the puddles!"

Winter

Rhymes

Snowflakes are falling, magically falling.
Snowflakes are falling, down to the ground.

Five little snow people standing on a hill,
Five little snow people standing very still.
The sun came out and melted one away.
Now there's four little snow people standing
there today (etc.).

Activities

- Cover pine cones with peanut butter and seeds.

- Make bird feeders out of plastic jugs and milk cartons.

- Take walks in the snow, listening for sounds and listening to the silence. Make shapes in the snow.

- Use your big toe as a pretend crayon, and draw snow people.

- Sitting down and using your arms as poles, ski down outstretched legs—whoosh!

Songs

Some songs to sing away the winter blues: "Shh, Be Quiet and Listen to the Snow," "Oh, It Snows and Blows at Wintertime," "See the Children Skating," "Jingle Bells."

Movement

- Vivaldi, "Winter," from "The Four Seasons": Start by sitting. To the steady beat of the music, rub arms, legs, hands, etc., to keep warm. As the music changes, flutter arms and fingers like snowflakes. The music alternates between rubbing and flutter. As the music becomes more fluid, add scarves, throwing them to the children, and stand up to celebrate the winter with Vivaldi.

- Strauss, "Skater's Waltz": Prerecord the music, with pauses. Skate around the room to the music. Working with a partner, build pretend snow people during each pause. Don't forget to put a hat way on top. With little ones, suggest the big bottom, tummy and head. What else do we need?

Spring

Rhymes

Spring has sprung, the sky is so blue.
The birdies are singing good morning to you.

Here's a little bunny, with ears so funny,
And here's her hole in the ground.
When a noise she hears, she perks up her ears
And jumps in her hole in the ground.

Activities

- Take a walk. Look very closely for signs of spring, using binoculars made of toilet-tissue holders. Use the binoculars as listening tubes to help you hear the birdies.

- Plant seeds, wash windows, clean out the flower beds.

Songs

Try: "Younger than Springtime," "Sing a Song of Springtime," "Say, Say, Oh Playmate," "Rain on the Green Grass," "Five Little Birds," "Way Up in the Sky," "Tiptoe through the Tulips."

Movement

- Some children are seeds, sleeping under the ground. Ask them what kinds of seeds they are. Other children are the sun, and others are the rain dancing around while the "seeds" start to grow. As the seeds slowly grow, there is a gentle breeze, etc. Ask the children to hold their shapes, and take a picture. What are they?

- "Spring," from Vivaldi's "The Four Seasons," lends itself to a simple spring dance.

Read More about Seasonal Celebrations

Carey, Diana, and Judy Large. *Festivals, Family and Food.* Stroud, U.K.: Hawthorn Press, 1986.

Filipiak, Susan. "Movement Ideas." Swing City Dance Studio, Ann Arbor, Mich.

Swinger, Marlys, ed. *Sing through the Seasons.* Robertsbridge, East Sussex: Plough Publishing House, 2000.

14

Play Parties and Singing Games

I hear and I forget. I see and I remember. I do and I understand.
—Chinese proverb

Children have to involve their bodies as well as their minds in order to understand the world and experiences. If he may not engage the body, as well as the mind, he will switch off.
—Sueann Robinson Ambron

What's a Play Party?

Mary Jeanette Howle explains what play parties are: "Play parties were multigenerational events in the rural areas and frontier regions of the United States during the 19th century. Play-party games filled a special niche at social events. The settlers desired some sort of entertainment at their gatherings, but did not allow dancing for religious reasons. Instrumental music, including fiddle music, was likewise prohibited because of its association with dancing." "Fiddles," according to Flora L. McDowell, "were sometimes referred to as the devil's instruments."

"To avoid the prohibited activities," Mary Jeanette Howle tells us, "the settlers developed play-party games, which did not require instruments. They used group movement and substituted simple steps for the intricate movements of the dance. In place of instrumental music, they used singing, hand clapping, and foot tapping to enable the members of the group to move together and make the activity more exciting and satisfying. The absence of instrumental accompaniment was the major distinction between play-party games and dances."

Happy Birthday

Perhaps a birthday party isn't an official play party, but here's a different song to sing on anyone's birthday, regardless of age:

Happy birthday, happy birthday. We love you.
Happy birthday, and may all your dreams
    come true.
When you blow out the candles, one light stays
    aglow.
That's the love light in your eyes where'er you go.
        (Tune: "Merry Widow Waltz")

Backyard Poetry

Here are some singing games that never go out of style.

Bouncing

One of my fondest childhood memories finds me on my driveway, chanting this ditty while throwing a ball at the side of the house:

Lean-zees, clap-zees, twirl-about, toe-bab-zees—
High-zees, low-zees, right hand, left hand—
Touch your head, touch your toes, under your
leg, and around you go—

Dorothy Mills Howard wrote about ball bouncing in 1949, explaining how much the activity contributes to a child's total development, allowing him or her to use both the mind and the body to coordinate and manipulate the ball along with the rhyme:

Very young children learning to bounce the ball use simple actions and rhythms: the bounce, catch, bounce, catch…The game is an individual one, with a few rare exceptions, and in its most elaborate forms approaches juggling…

All the rhythmic body movements that accompany the bouncing ball cannot be seen or heard, for the process involves the whole nervous system….Visual experiences clearly play a part in the rhythm…

In ball bouncing play, the rhythm of the rhymes and the body are one….The child chants his rhyme as a part of a larger pattern that involves all parts of his body sensuously integrated with the ball movements and other objects and sights in the worlds about him.

The voice is employed in many ways to make a rhyme fit the desired actions. The child's voice does unaccountable tricks with words. Not only do children adjust syllables to meet ball and body movements but they also give sound effects to please their unappraised and unconscious needs for melody and euphony.

Thus onomatopoeia, one of the oldest tricks known to language and poetry, is employed unconsciously by children in a folk art which is a part of the cultural inheritance of children the world over.

There is evidence that the ball-bouncing games of children today are folk activities with ancient lineage.…The earliest literature of the world makes mention of the ball.

Mary Austin explains: "Rhythm develops, and the skeletal muscles play a part in development… [of] the autonomic nervous system, together with and inseparable from the intellect.…The form is the resulting coordination of the individual with his whole environment of animate and inanimate things." Ales Hrdlicka adds that "rhythm can be defined as motor music," while Louis Untermeyer calls rhythm "the base of poetry because it is the fundamental principle of life."

"The rhythms of nature," Dorothy Mills Howard says, "were one with man for a hundred thousand years before intelligence began to direct his conduct. The baby beats his toys with some regularity, accompanied by many movements of the body. The child, chanting a rhyme, sets up a train of sound waves in the air: the sound goes out to listeners and returns to the child, a listener, arousing ideas and emotions by which the child links himself with a rhythmic world."

Children's play rhymes and customs flow down the years of history; they are a part of the natural poetry of childhood, and they become part of who we are as adults. Every summer I attend a festival celebrating traditional music with several thousand folks. Last year I was waiting in line at the ice cream booth when two young men with camp T-shirts came to make a purchase. The older woman behind the stand asked the young men what their favorite camp song was. They immediately broke into song, she joining them, and before long a crowd of strangers had united by sharing a childhood favorite together.

Clapping and Chanting

My years at camp implanted songs and chants that often involve rhythmic hand clapping with a partner or clapping hands with the person next to you in a circle. I can't guarantee that these are the exact words—just how I recall them. Make up your own melodies and hand gestures, or contact me for a reconstruction.

Chickens and Hens

Who stole my chickens and my hens?
Whock-a-do, whock-a-do, whock-a-do.
Who stole my chickens and my hens?
Whock-a-do, whock-a-do, whock-a-do.
Who stole my chickens?
Who stole my hens?
Who stole my chickens and my hens?

Fee Fly (Each word or phrase is echoed)

Fee—fee fly—fee fly floo—
Kum-a-lotta, kum-a-lotta, kum-a-lotta, vee stah—
Oh no no no not the vee stah—
Hex-a-meeny, hex-a-meeny, ooh walla-walla
*   meeney—*
Des-a-meeney hey-a-meeny, ooh walla-wah—
Zip-did de-de-oh-do, dee-oh-do, dee-oh-do—
Zip-did de-oh-do, dee-oh-do, shhhhhhh.

Onni Wonni

Ah-ooo, ah-ooo
Ah-ooo-knee woo-knee wha-ah ooo-knee
Ah-ooo-knee woo-knee wha-ah ooo-knee
Aye yi-yi yippee-yi ki-ay
Miss-aye yi-yi yippee-yi ki-ay
A-oon ah-ooo-knee key-chee.

Yodeler on a Mountain So High

Oh there once was a yodeler on a mountain so
*   high,*
When along came a cuckoo bird interrupting
*   his cry.*
Ho-leeee-aaah,
Ho-lee-ah, cu-kee-ah, ho-lee-ah cuckoo,
Ho-lee-ah, cu-kee-ah, ho-lee-ah cuckoo,
Ho-lee-ah, cu-kee-ah, ho-lee-ah cuckoo,
Ho-lee-ah, cu-kee-ah, ooooh.[14]

Active Singing versus Ordinary Games

Why sing actively as part of play? What are the benefits? Consider the following:

- Children are least auditory: their experiences need to also be both visual and kinesthetic.

Singing games provide:

- An introduction to poetry
- Sequence, as a child shifts from solitary to cooperative play
- A link between early songs and beginning reading skills
- Easy learning and remembering through the three Rs: rhyme, repetition and rhythm
- Support for a child's sequential development of gross motor skills
- A vehicle for learning: movement nourishes brain development
- Practice at following simple rules
- Opportunities to improve listening skills
- A chance to feel comfortable moving through space
- A safe environment where children can make mistakes
- A chance to understand other cultures

[14] See http://www.boyscouttrail.com/boy-scouts/boy-scout-songs.asp for the rest of the words and motions.

- Children need to experience the joy of discovery through play.

- Children are wired for movement: it energizes them and relieves stress.

- These games give children practice with social skills and taking turns.

- Many of these games are played in a circle, giving everyone equal status.

- These games are based on coordination of mind, voice and body, building both musical and social know-how.

- Active learning takes place when a game is new to a child.

- The games' words provide a model of complete sentences and may introduce new parts of speech in an easy and enjoyable way.

- Such activities bring people together, building a sense of community.

- These games give children a chance to celebrate their heritage and diverse ethnic backgrounds.

- These games help soothe a cranky soul, build trust and self-esteem and are a safe vehicle for self-expression.

Some Examples of Singing Games

- "All around the Kitchen"
- "The Bear Went over the Mountain"
- "BINGO"
- "Bow, Belinda"
- "The Grand Old Duke of York"
- "Going Down the Alley, Sally"
- "In and Out the Window"
- "Jump Jim Joe"
- "The Mexican Hat Dance"
- "All around the Mulberry Bush"
- "On the Mountain"
- "Rig-a-Jig-Jig"
- "Shoo Fly"
- "Skip to My Lou"

A great deal of learning takes place during singing games.

- Children learn melodies and perform actions that reinforce musical rhythms phrases.
- Children improve their listening skills: they must listen for a change in the music to change their movements.
- Once children know a game, they will anticipate its next movement with their bodies.
- Children learn to share and take turns, developing their social skills.
- Children can alter the activities to meet new occasions or moods.
- Children expand their knowledge of other times and cultures, enriching their lives.

Learn More about Play Parties and Singing Games

Austin, Mary. *The American Rhythm.* New York: 1930.

Howle, Mary Jeanette. "Play Party Games in the Modern Classroom." *MENC Journal* (March 1997).

Hrdlicka, Ales. *Children Who Run on All Fours.* New York: 1930.

Jones, Bessie. *Put Your Hand on Your Hip and Let Your Backbone Slip: Songs and Games from the Georgia Sea Islands.* Burlington, Mass.: Rounder Records, 2001.

Jones, Bessie, and Bess Lomax Hawes. *Step It Down: Games, Play Songs and Stories in the Afro-American Heritage.* Athens: University of Georgia Press, 1987.

Trinka, Jill. *Folk Songs, Singing Games, and Play Parties for Kids of All Ages.* Series of four books and tapes. Chicago: GIA Publications.

Untermeyer, Louis. *Forms of Poetry.* New York: 1936.

Additional Song Resources

Beachnet: http://www.beachnet.com/'jeanettem/chants.html.

Boy Scout Trail: http://www.boyscouttrail.com/boy-scouts/boy-scout-songs.asp.

National Children's Folksong Repository: http://www.edu-cyberpg.com/NCFR/collect.html. (This site contains links to many other folk songs and chants. You can also share your song: call toll-free, 877-220-0262.)

"Somewhere Over the Rainbow: The Wizard of Oz Homepage": http://www.home.att.net/~wizardoz/.

"Who Stole My Chickens and My Eggs?": http://dragon.sleepdeprived.ca/songbook/songs3/S3_84.htm. (This site also has a version of accompanying actions.)

YouTube: http://www.youtube.com/ (Type in the name of any song to find lyrics and often a recorded version.)

SO MANY BOOKS...SO LITTLE TIME...

15

Parents, teachers & librarians must get to know the books currently available for children—especially the available books that children absolutely adore.
—**Mem Fox,** *Radical Reflections*

Oh the places you'll go. There is fun to be done.
—**Dr. Seuss,** *Oh, the Places You'll Go!*

It's hard to read about child development without seeing the words "emergent literacy" and "early literacy" appear over and over. Many early childhood programs and public schools are using "early literacy" to push reading and writing skills on little ones, often before it may be developmentally appropriate.

Reading to children from very early on, of course, is wonderful for babies and can impact their love of books forever. But if the focus is only on teaching them to read and write, we may be losing sight of the bigger picture. Unless children are at risk, for whatever reason, most will learn to read and write when their brains are ready.

Also, according to the American Library Association, several studies point to a relationship between reading together and the emotional development of young children. A simple picture book, in other words, can help strengthen the bond between child and caregiver. And children's author Mem Fox tells us "that learning to read and learning to love reading owe a great deal (much more than we ever dreamed) to the nature of the human relationships that occur around and through books."

So read, read, read, read, to your little ones every day. You'll be providing an environment in which children will learn to love sounds, rhythms and captivating illustrations. And perhaps just as important, the time you spend reading together will build a treasured and lasting relationship.

Libraries Are Special Places

In many communities, the library is a central meeting place. Story times are free and open to everyone. Families can gather at the library, make new friends, form play groups. Librarians thus have a unique opportunity to provide resources: lists of books, articles about literacy and child development, notice of area events. When people move to a new community, they often look to the librarian as a source of comfort and familiarity in a strange and sometimes overwhelming environment. I always suggest to librarians who lead story times to save a block of time at the end for families to chat while the children play. It can make a huge difference in their lives.

Story Time Picture Book Discussions

Another way to involve children in story time is to have book discussions. Basically, the goal is to get the children thinking—how, what, when, why—and comparing situations in the story to their own lives. Here are some suggestions for lead-in questions that could apply to any story.[15]

1. Do you think —— has/have ever —— before?

2. The —— was/were —— (e.g., afraid) of many things in the story. Would you be scared of any of those things?

3. What do/does the —— think is going to happen to them when they ——? What really happens?

4. What helps the —— not to feel ——? What helps you feel —— when you are ——?

5. Was there a pattern in this story? Can you tell me something about it?

6. What was the sequence of events in the story? What did the —— do first? Next? Last?

7. Can you think of some rhyming words that were used in this story?

8. Can you think of some action words that were used in this story?

9. Would the book have been as good without the pictures?

10. How would you describe the pictures (big/small/colorful/dark/fun/serious)?

11. How would you describe —— (character's) (color, clothing, personality)?

12. What kind of "medium" did the artist use?

13. Do you think that the —— had fun on their adventure?

14. What kind of adventures do you like?

Books to Love

Starting with Classics

Ludwig Bemelmans, *Madeline*

Raymond Briggs, *The Snowman*

Don Freeman, *Corduroy*

Crockett Johnson, *Harold and the Purple Crayon*

Ezra Jack Keats, *The Snowy Day*

Robert McCloskey, *Make Way for Ducklings*

What Parents and Caregivers Can Do

- Begin reading as soon as baby is born, if not sooner.
- Reread favorite books again and again.
- Repeat strings of sound ("bah bah bah bah") and add to them.
- Take a daily walk, and name objects in the environment.
- Talk about daily, routine activities.
- Make the time to listen with sincere interest.
- Draw attention to print in everyday settings.
- Introduce new words.
- Read poetry.
- Occasionally point to words and pictures as you read.
- Provide a variety of materials for scribbling and drawing.
- Write down children's stories.
- Help children dictate and decorate letters.
- Provide opportunities to experiment with reading and writing when children appear ready.
- Read out loud every day.

[15] Thank you to Jayne Damron, from the Farmington Community Library, and Angela Semifero, from the Marshall District Library, both in Michigan, for these discussion ideas.

Watty Piper, *The Little Engine That Could*

Beatrix Potter, *Tales of Peter Rabbit*

The Real Mother Goose (Checkerboard Press)

H. A. Rey, *Curious George*

Maurice Sendak, *Nutshell Library*

Esphyr Slobodkina, *Caps for Sale*

Simple and Sweet

Martha Alexander, *"A" You're Adorable*

Kathy Henderson, *Bumpety Bump*

Judy Hindley, *Eyes, Nose, Fingers and Toes*

Susan Meyer, *Everywhere Babies*

Mary Murphy, *I Kissed the Baby!*

Helen Oxenbury, *All Fall Down, Clap Hands,* and *Say Goodnight*

Betty Ann Schwartz, *What Makes a Rainbow?*

Ann Taylor, *Baby Dance* (and several others)

Sing a Story

Kathi Appelt, *Oh My Baby, Little One*

Tedd Arnold, *Catalina Magdelena*

Mem Fox, *Time for Bed*

Bill Martin Jr., *Brown Bear, Brown Bear, What Do You See?* and *Listen to the Rain*

Dugald Steer, *Snappy Little Farmyard*

Sue Williams, *I Went Walking*

Simple Sounds

Alex Ayliffe, *Slither, Swoop, Swing*

Arline L. Bronzaft, *Listen to the Raindrops*

Denise Fleming, *Barnyard Banter* and *In the Tall Tall Grass*

Tomie de Paola, *Mice Squeak, We Speak*

Sheena Roberts, *We All Go Traveling By*

Sing-Aong

Jane Cabrera, *Over in the Meadow*

Geoffrey Hayes, *The Ants Go Marching*

Steven Kellogg, *A-Hunting We Will Go!*

Sylvia Long, *Twinkle, Twinkle, Little Star*

Bob Merrill, *How Much Is That Doggie in the Window?*

Pamela Paparone, *Five Little Ducks*

Melissa Sweet, *Fiddle-I-Fee*

Iza Trapani, *Row Row Row Your Boat* and *Shoo Fly* (and several others)

Rosemary Wells, *I Love You a Bushel and a Peck*

Sing, Skip and Scat

Karen Beaumont, *I Ain't Gonna Paint No More!*

Joy Cowley, *Nicketty-Nacketty Noo-Noo-Noo*

Melanie Davis Jones, *Pigs Rock!*

Bonnie Lass and Philemon Sturges, *Who Took the Cookies from the Cookie Jar?*

Bill Martin Jr., *The Maestro Plays*

Joyce Maxner, *Nicholas Cricket*

C. M. Millen, *Blue Bowl Down*

Tony Mitton, *Down by the Cool of the Pool*

Ellen Olson-Brown and Brian Claflin, *Bake You a Pie*

Chris Raschka, *Charlie Parker Played Be-Bop*

Carole Boston Weatherford, *Jazz Baby*

Story Books

Dori Chaconas, *On a Wintry Morning*

Trish Cooke, *Full, Full, Full of Love* and *So Much*

Rachel Isadora, *Peekaboo Morning*

Nancy Shaw, *Raccoon Tune* (and several others)

Toby Speed, *Hattie Baked a Wedding Cake*

Simms Taback, *Joseph Had a Little Overcoat*

Margaret Wild, *Our Granny*

Strike Up the Band

A. G. Dening, *Who Is Tapping at My Window?*

Woody Guthrie, *Bling-Blang*

B. G. Hennessy, *Jake Baked the Cake*

Nancy Van Laan, *Possum Come A-Knockin'*

Linda Williams, *The Little Old Lady Who Was Not Afraid of Anything*

Strrrretch

Eric Carle, *From Head to Toe*

Rachel Carr, *Be a Frog, a Bird or a Tree*

Doreen Cronin, *Wiggle*

Jonathan London, *Wiggle Waggle*

Jean Marzollo and Jerry Pinkney, *Pretend You're a Cat*

Suggesting Movement

Margaret Wise Brown, *The Runaway Bunny*

Rod Campbell, *Dear Zoo*

Eric Carle, *Papa, Please Get the Moon for Me*

Lois Ehlert, *Waiting for Wings*

Keith Faulkner, *The Wide-Mouthed Frog*

Mirra Ginsburg, *Mushroom in the Rain*

Robert Kalan, *Jump Frog Jump*

Jonathan London, *Froggy Gets Dressed*

Sail Away

Joan Blos, *Bedtime!*

Margaret Wise Brown, *Home for a Bunny*

Jon Butler and Susan Schade, *I Love You, Good Night*

Mem Fox, *Time for Bed*

Jonathan London, *Snuggle Wuggle* and *What Do You Love*

Sylvia Long, *Hush Little Baby*

Jane Simmons, *Go to Sleep, Daisy*

Hope Vestergaard, *Hillside Lullaby*

Audrey Wood, *Piggies*

Speaking of Art and Poetry

Giles Andreae, *Giraffes Can't Dance*

Karen Beaumont, *Baby Danced the Polka*

Joan Blos, *A Seed a Flower a Minute, an Hour*

Bruce Degen, *Jamberry*

Eloise Greenfield, *Water, Water*

Bill Grossman, *My Little Sister Ate One Hare*

A. A. Milne, *The World of Christopher Robin*

Tomie de Paola, *The Legend of the Indian Paintbrush*

Malvina Reynolds, *Morningtown Ride*

Peter H. Reynolds, *The Dot*

Cindy Rink, *Where Does the Wind Blow?*

Alison Sage, ed., *Treasury of Children's Poetry*

Rosemary Wells, *Carry Me!*

Audrey Wood, *Silly Sally*

Read More about Literature

Crawford, Patricia A. "Reading the Rainbow: Exploring Color Concepts through Picture Books." *Focus on Pre-K and K* 20, no. 3 (2008).

Gauthier, Delores R. "Children's Literature in the Music Classroom: Finding the Music Within." *MENC Journal* (January 2005).

Martin, Kathleen. "What's in a Name?" *Focus on Pre-K and K* 21, no. 2 (2008).

McDonald, Margaret Read. *Shake-It-Up Tales!* Little Rock: August House, 2000.

Strasser, Janis, and Holly Seplocha. "Using Picture Books to Support Young Children's Literacy." *Childhood Education* (Summer 2007).

Williams, Lunetta, M. Hedrick, and Wanda B. Tuschinski. "Motivation: Going beyond Testing to a Lifetime of Reading." *Childhood Education* (Spring 2008).

Associations and Online Resources>

American Library Association: http://www.ala.org.

Every Child Ready to Read: http://www.pla.org/ala/alsc/ECRR/ECRRHomePage.htm.

Grow Up Reading: http://www.growupreading.org.

KidsReads.com: http://www.kidsreads.com.

Mazza Museum: International Art from Picture Books: http://www.findlay.edu/offices/resources/mazza/default.htm.

Robert Munsch: http://www.robertmunsch.com.

FOR ART'S SAKE

Imagination is more important than knowledge.
—Albert Einstein

Winter is an etching, Spring a watercolor,
Summer an oil painting, and Autumn a mosaic of them all.
—Stanley Horowitz

Scribbling leads very clearly and directly toward developing the
ability to read and write.
—**Susan Striker,** *Young at Art*

Young children need lots of opportunities every day to process art—toddlers too. Whether at home or in the classroom, always have materials available allowing children to explore and create. Working with different materials gives children a vehicle for self-expression and can also help them focus, create, think and get in touch with who they are, not who we tell them to be.

We may confuse making art with art "projects," where adults precut designs and instruct children where or how to paint or paste. By precutting, we're doing children's work for them. In the classroom, avoid "parent pleasers": projects where the children's work is lined up, all looking very similar in content. Most cities have recycling centers where items can be picked up free or for a nominal cost. Have paints, crayons, paste, scissors, feathers, pipe cleaners, fabric, wallpaper, wood, leaves, sticks, clay, sponges, brushes, etc., around for children to do a little or a lot. Let children mix paints.

Art is a natural extension of a young child's development. Provide materials just for art's sake, to extend story time, to enhance science and music activities. Children need to manipulate materials and create their own works of art without guidelines from grown-ups. They can decide if they want to put their name on the work or not, and they might choose to take their work home or to find a spot to display it.

There's More to Art than Meets the Eye

Johanna Graine Mabry, a clinical social worker and registered art therapist, tells me that "it is helpful if parents/caregivers identify their own issues around creativity and find ways to inspire their children without using direct praise or having expectations for a physical outcome to their process. Adults can spend time scanning themselves during art experiences with their children—do they have any anxiety about messiness, expectation, frustrations, etc. Are they relaxed, tense, rushing through the time, and so on. The presence of any feeling can indicate that they may have issues to be aware of. We all do. The important thing is to know they are present and to find ways to work around them (while working on them). If paint in the house is stressful, do not try to do it: sign up for a class or paint outside in good weather versus trying to do something that feels terrible. But it is important for the adult to explore how to work on letting go of what makes painting tense. They must work diligently on letting go of the need for an outcome. Art: it is a process, not for [a] product!"

Mabry points out that "early art experiences make an unconscious imprint on our emotional and cognitive selves that can impact us throughout our life span. Having a trusted adult judge our early work can have negative consequences in so many areas of our lives. The creative process is often one that involves problem solving, and if we are not given the necessary opportunities to problem solve in a positive and supportive environment, then our creative abilities in various aspects of our lives can be stifled. Just as we learn from our infant years to build secure, trusting attachments, so too do we learn about our creative abilities by how those around us react to our early experiments with creative exploration. If as youngsters we are not given the freedom and encouragement to express without judgment, then we are bound to seek and need the approval of others and often become resistant to expressing freely what is truly unique and unguarded in the future."

I asked Mabry what to say to toddlers' caregivers who want to show their children how to draw or to label their drawings. She replied:

Toddlers are not at a developmental phase where drawing pictures that resemble reality is important. Parents should be encouraged to allow their child to draw freely, and if they must interact with them, they could ask them open-ended questions coupled with nonjudgmental comments like, 'I see you are working

hard. I see lines, color, movement and texture. I wonder what you see,' versus 'Is that a monkey?' or 'What is it?' Drawing pictures for your children or showing them how to draw something limits their creative resources and sets unrealistic expectations. Even the most persistent youth saying, 'Mommy, please draw me a cat,' can be redirected so that they take the lead with the experience. A parent could brainstorm out loud, 'Ummm, let's see. How would we draw a cat?' Pause. 'Well, does the cat have different parts to it?' Pause. Wait for the child to respond. 'What are those parts, and can you think of shapes that might remind you of those parts?' Then the parent could begin to encourage the child to draw the spaces and compose the image in the way they wish, using out-loud problem solving, all while the parent never touches the paper! This method requires work on the parent's part and is not the easiest and simplest way to get a drawing done. But it is the creative way that enriches the child's self-concept, builds self-esteem, and is free of any judgment. This is where parents must always remind themselves of their own issues: Are they really wanting to play right now, or are they thinking about their work that needs to get done? Are they having some frustrations come up with their child that might be getting in the way of them being present for the child's process? Do they have unrealistic expectations of their abilities?

Johanna Graine Mabry, Clinical Social Worker and Registered Art Therapist—Ann Arbor, Michigan

Wow. Mabry's words sum it all up for me, and her wisdom has helped me enormously when I play with my own grandchildren. This is advice that money can't buy.

Helping All Children Reach Their Full Artistic Potential, at Home or in the Classroom

Please do:

- Be aware of how you react to children's art-work. Refrain from making comments or judgments about art work. Remind children that there is no right or wrong way to create images and that all products are important.

- Make observations about the image produced. Say, "I see lines, straight and curvy."

- Serve as a witness or observer of the creative process. You can provide assistance with materials (without doing the task for the child) and be a support when issues surface.

- Experiment with art materials before presenting them to children. You will feel more confident when you know the materials and techniques. Be aware of how the materials can affect the art-making process.

- Lose your expectations. Let the child explore and problem-solve with the materials. The act of squeezing the glue may be more important to a child than pasting the tissue paper on the page. Always remember: it's the process that's important, not the product, and it's your child's experience, not yours!

- Be aware of your control issues with messiness—we all have them. Think about how you will manage your impulses to straighten, clean, organize.

- Remember that children will be spontaneous in their creative process. Some may choose a material and allow the product to develop. Others will have an idea and seek out materials to create the product. Provide opportunities for children to approach image-making in whatever way feels safe and comfortable.

- Always approach the child's artwork with respect. Inform the child if you are going to touch or move it. Always try to keep the images the child creates. Create a portfolio to store your child's work (twenty by twenty-four inches is a great size). Once the child has shown or stated that she or he is done with an activity, allow some time for the two of you to silently look at the image together. As the child gets older (three or three and a half), she or he may begin to tell you the story behind an image as you look on quietly. Younger children will usually not recognize their work soon after they finish. They will often not recall the thoughts and feelings they had during the process. Remember that toddlers are more interested in the process—exploring the materials and using their bodies to create.

- Follow the child's lead. If your child says, "Look, a train," you can explore the aspects of the image in nonjudgmental ways. Keep in mind that the same picture could become a boat two hours later—just remember to let the child lead you in the discussion. If the child is using a metaphor, make sure you stay in that metaphor.

Please don't:

- Give a child coloring books. Turn those children's menus over so children can explore with their own imaginations.

- Make too many comments during the child's process

- Use praise: "What pretty lines," "Good job," "You're great."

- Draw, paint or write on your child's image or show your child how to draw. This can inhibit her or his creative development.

- Interfere or correct a child if he or she is using

material in an "improper" way (unless it's not safe)

- Suggest themes: "Paint me a train."

- Let the child see you throw out any creation

The Creative Space: Environment and Materials

- Create a place in your home that is dedicated to creative explorations. The space should be accessible, and caregivers should be prepared for it to get messy.

- Provide adequate space to allow for spontaneous movement to occur while children are engaged in image-making. If possible, have an adjustable double-sided easel available with fresh paper.

- Paint should be in non-spill pots, with color-coordinated brushes on one side of the easel and drawing materials (crayons, chalk, markers, etc.) on the other side. If you don't have an easel, tape paper across the top of a child-size table or on the floor. Small cat dishes are great for floor/table paint pots (bowls with weighted bases mean fewer spills).

- Provide child-size furniture whenever possible. Tables and chairs need to be comfortable and inviting. The space and furniture should allow for messiness, including possible spills and damage.

- Safety should always be maintained and respected. Always work in well-ventilated rooms, use nontoxic materials and be aware of smells. Paint is very slippery, so plan ahead if you're using it on the floor.

- Provide well-maintained materials. Check them frequently, and replace broken or extremely worn items.

- Keep material well-organized and visible to the child. (If the child is under two, materials could be placed out of reach but within sight.)

- Use high-quality materials.

- Use heavyweight paper (white: seventy-eighty-pound paper; fadeless construction: eighty-eighty-five-pound paper.). Use paper that's at least eleven by fourteen inches (at least arm's length).

- Don't use precut paper that resembles something or paper that has images on it that could be distracting.

- Provide materials that are multicultural: crayons, markers, colored paper, yarns, paints, collage pictures, etc.

- Be aware of clean-up procedures, and have fun cleaning up. Young children can enjoy washing a brush in soapy water as much as they enjoy the creative process.

Read More about Art

Bos, Bev. "Don't Move the Muffin Tins." Turn the Page Press. http://www.turnthepage.com.

Brashears, Deya. *Dribble Drabble.* Colorado: DME Publications, 1985.

Epstein, Ann S. *Supporting Young Artists: The Development of the Visual Arts in Young Children.* Ypsilanti, Mich.: High/Scope Press, 2002.

Loomis, Kathleen, Catharine Lewis, and Rachel Blumenthal. "Children Learn to Think and Create through Art." *Young Children* (September 2007).

Striker, Susan. *Please Touch: How to Stimulate Your Child's Creative Development through Movement, Music, Art, and Play.* New York: Simon and Schuster, 1986.

Striker, Susan. *Young at Art.* New York: Henry Holt and Co, 2001.

Van't Hul, Jean. "Big Hands, Small Art: Whether It's Finger Painting or Collage, Creative Self-Expression Abounds in a Toddler Art Group." *Mothering Magazine* (July–August 2007).

Winner, Ellen, and Lois Hetland. "Art for Our Sake: School Arts Classes Matter More Than Ever—But Not for the Reasons You Think." 2007.
http://www.boston.com/news/globe/ideas/articles/2007/09/02/art_for_our_sake/.

The Conductor

TO GARI

IT'S VERY

NICE TO

SEE YOU.

THANK

YOU FOR

THE

MUSIC.

LOVE,

JULIAN

LOVE EMMA
THANK YOU FOR
BEIG MY MUSIC
TEACKER

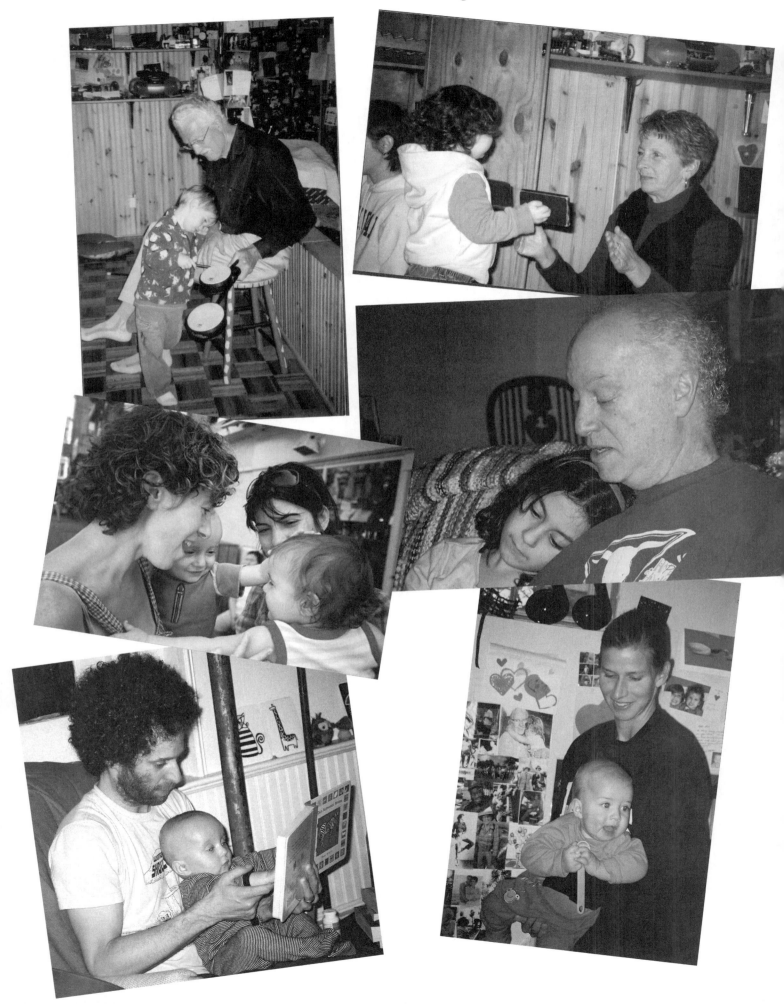

17

LULLABY AND GOOD NIGHT

Hush a bye, don't you cry.
Go to sleepy little baby.
When you wake, you shall have
All the pretty little horses.
Black and bay, dapple and gray,
Coach and six white horses.
—Traditional song, South Carolina

Lullabies are not just for babies. Settling down, cheek to cheek, head to heart, benefits everyone, young and old and in-between. One of my fondest memories is of the closeness of my mother's breath and the rhythm of her heartbeat as she sang my favorite lullabies—back and forth, back and forth. Rocking back and forth and side to side nourishes the brain, helps bring calm and is very satisfying.

I often well up with emotion when I end music time with a lullaby. Even my six-year-old granddaughter still likes to snuggle with me in the rocking chair, her legs hanging over the edge, as we share our favorites.

One day a grandma accompanied her daughter and granddaughter to class. After I suggested that participants "find someone to cuddle," I looked over. Do you know what that grandma was doing? She was holding her daughter, who was holding her own daughter. It was an enormously moving moment that will stay with me forever.

At music time, if children are without a grown-up, I tell them to rock their pretend babies. And so it goes: we rock, we sing and we find a moment of peace and serenity.

One night, my granddaughter, about age two, was having a sleepover—or rather a sleepless sleepover—and the only thing that helped was the lullaby "Go to Sleepy, Baby-Bye." I sang it over and over and over and over, at least one hundred times, substituting the names of everyone she knew, including her dog. My voice growing hoarse, I dared not stop, as the music kept her calm and relaxed, finally taking her back to dreamland.

Sail-Away Songs and Rhymes

Go to Sleepy, Baby-Bye (South Carolina)
Go to sleepy, baby-bye. Go to sleepy, baby-bye.
Mama's gone to the mail boat, Papa's gone to
*   the mail boat, bye.*
Bye oh baby-bye. Bye oh baby-bye.
(Name's) gone to the mail boat, bye.

Golden Slumbers (Thomas Dekker)
Golden slumbers kiss your eyes.
Smiles awake you when you rise.
Sleep little darling, do not cry,
And I will sing a lullaby.

Cares you know, not there for sleep,
While I o'er you watch do keep.
Sleep little darling, do not cry,
And I will sing a lullaby.

Baby's Boat's a Silver Moon (source unknown)

Baby's boat's a silver moon
Floating through the sky
Sailing oe'r the sea of sleep
While the clouds roll by.
Sail baby, sail, out upon that sea,
Only don't forget to sail home again to me.

Baby's wishing for a dream, wishing near and far.
Her line's a silver moonbeam, her bait's a silver
    star.
Sail baby, sail, out upon that sea,
Only don't forget to sail home again to me.

Tender Shepherd (Jule Charlap and Mark Styne)

Tender shepherd, tender shepherd,
Let me help you count your sheep.
One in the meadow, two in the garden,
Three safe and happily fall asleep.

Tender shepherd, tender shepherd,
You forgot to count your sheep.
One, climb the stairs, and two, say your
    prayers,
and three, safe and happily fall asleep.

Sleep, Little One, Sleep (traditional)

Sleep, little one, sleep.
Out of doors there runs a sheep
A sheep with four white feet
That drinks its milk so sweet,
Sleep, little one, sleep.
In the woods there runs a spotted cow.
Its calf has shut its eyelids now.
Sleep, baby, sleep.

Dance to Your Daddy (traditional)

Dance to your daddy, my little laddie.
Dance to your daddy, my bonnie lamb.
You shall have a fishy in your little dishy.
You shall have a fishy when the boat comes in.

You shall have an apple, you shall have a plum,
You shall have a rattle when your daddy comes.
You shall have an apple, you shall have a plum,
You shall have a rattle when your daddy comes.

Bye-o my baby,
Bye-o my baby,
Bye-o baby, don't you cry.
Bye-o, my baby,
B-O, bye-o baby,
B-O, bye-o baby, bye-o baby bye.

This Little Wind (blowing on fingers)

This little wind blows silver rain.
This little wind drifts snow.
This little wind sings a whistle tune.
This little wind moans low.
But this little wind rocks baby birds
Tenderly to and fro.

By'm Bye

By'm bye. By'm bye.
Stars shining, number, number one,
Number two, number three, number four,
Number five, oh my.
By'm bye, b'm bye, oh my.
By'm bye.

Lullaby for Teddy-O (Douglas Mountain)

Sleep my teddy-o.
Let all your worries go.
I'm here for you,
Near for you.
Sleep my teddy-o.
The day has come to end.
The moon it is my friend.
The darkness creeps.
The mountains sleep.
And so does teddy-O.
The orange sun has set.
The grass is cool and wet.

There's peace for miles.
The river smiles
And so does teddy-O.

Wiggle Wiggle, Fingers
Wiggle wiggle, fingers, waaay up to the sky.
Wiggle wiggle fingers. Wave them all goodbye.

Sail-Away Songs

Various artists, *For Our Children: Tenth Anniversary Edition* (Kid Rhino)

Judy Garland, *Somewhere over the Rainbow*[16]

Gemini, *Lullabies for Our Children* (Gemini)

Priscilla Herdman, *Stardreamer: Nightsongs and Lullabies* (Alcazar)

Golden Slumbers: A Father's Lullaby (Warner Brothers)

Kenny Loggins, *Return to Pooh Corner* (Sony Wonder)

[16] To hear Judy Garland, go to http://home.att.net/~wizardoz/overtherainbow.wav.]

Love Is All Around

Authentic Children's Music by Authentic Children's Musicians

If music be the food of love, play on.
—**William Shakespeare**, *Twelfth Night*

18

In September of 2007 I attended my first annual national conference of the Children's Music Network (CMN). This gathering was also a celebration of the organization's twenty years serving children and their families. CMN was started by folks like Pete Seeger, who, according to CMN's mission statement, "cared about the quality and content of children's music and recognize children's music as a powerful means of encouraging cooperation, celebrating diversity, building self-esteem, promoting respect and responsibility for our environment and cultivating understanding of nonviolence and social justice."

I have been attending various conferences for over twenty years, but never have I experienced one like this. Almost every one of the over two hundred people in attendance are accomplished songwriters and performers. Most are professional musicians, but many have other "day" jobs in addition to music. The group was welcoming and generous beyond belief. Although many of its members have known each other for twenty years, they included me in the group within minutes.

From Friday evening until Sunday afternoon, I had the gift of hearing song after song that celebrated childhood and families. I met talented and gifted musicians willing to share and collaborate. The energy was like being at a church revival, campfire sing-along and football rally—all at the same time. Voices and hearts joined together in harmony, tears flowed, and for a short time, love truly made the world go around.

Upon my return, it literally took me over two weeks to catch up on my sleep and get back to teaching without being in a daze. I cannot adequately put into words the spirit of this overwhelming experience. Each and every one of the people whom I spoke with communicated a vision to make this world a better place through their music. I witnessed again and again how one person can help cultivate change and the power of a group to help implement that change.

Although I was at a personal point of slight frustration, not yet having this book finished, this turned out to be a blessing: it would have been a sad omission not to include the work of these accomplished, fabulous, professional musicians—regular everyday folks, taking care of their families, some making a living with their music and some just trying to get by.

It is with great pride that I present the following musicians, each of whom manages to capture the essence of childhood and family. I asked them all to share their first musical memory, to talk about why they do what they do, to explain the impact music has on the lives of young children and their families—or to contribute anything at all about their philosophies.

Because of You, There's a Song in My Heart

Dancing with your feet is one thing, but dancing with your heart is another.

Lisa Atkinson, San Mateo, California

I consider it a privilege and an honor to be able to come into a room and share music and stories that have touched my heart. It is always a new experience, even if I've sung that particular song ten thousand times. I love to see and hear children I've sung with as babies growing up as vibrant human beings and have them mention in a hug, a song or a smile that my music had something to do with their being able to deal with the world around them. Now if that would just pay the rent…yup, we gotta work on that.

Along with my three titles on "A Gentle Wind," I am very proud to finally release on CD a collection of songs that came out of many songwriting workshops over the last twenty years. *Something to Sing About* is now available at CDbaby.com. Many fine Santa Cruz musicians make this a collection I am very proud of.

Find Lisa's music at http://www.atkinsonkincheloe.com and http://www.cdbaby.com.

Joni AvRutick, South Burlington, Vermont

Singing is transforming. I have always loved to sing, and while I'm not a particularly gifted singer, I experience the magic that the vibrations create. Singing together builds community. It provides another venue for self-expression and inclusion. As a preschool and elementary school teacher, music is a core part of my classroom. We march, we skip, we pause, we clap to create and accentuate rhythm. We sing songs that tell stories, give information or pass on historical events. We sing silly songs, folk songs, popular songs, rounds, topical songs and original songs. We add on to and change lyrics of familiar songs to personalize them and include ourselves in the living world of folk music.

As a songwriter, I have always been drawn to rhyme and meter. I delight in the cleverness of a fitting or silly rhyme. Children feel seen, heard and valued when they can freely contribute to a song and have their ideas sung back by the group. More than anything else I hope to model a love of music that is fun and inviting!

Joni teaches first and second grade at the Schoolhouse in South Burlington, Vermont. She is a songwriter who performs music for children and families with her musical partner, Gigi Weisman. She is currently working with Gigi on a CD of some of her original songs called In a Tree. *Contact Joni atjavrutick@yahoo.com.*

Judy Bayse, Sunnyvale, California

I was teaching a group of fifth-graders about songwriting, and we were also learning about the Underground Railroad. The kids had some interesting topics they wanted to write about—we ended up with one about Barbie and Ken (and Barbie's superficiality) and one about the importance of friends and how they accept you as you are.

Well, I got inspired to write a song about what each of us might have done if we were around during the times of slavery, whether we would've stepped up to help. I called it

"Northbound Train." The kids enjoyed it, and especially loved joining in on the backup parts. We ended up doing it in an assembly with 120 fourth- and fifth-graders singing my song.

They also sang spirituals and work songs with such commitment and, dare I say, spirituality. I think they truly felt the power of these songs after learning their history. It was a memorable performance, and many teachers came by to tell me they had tears in their eyes. It was an example of why I do what I do, and the power of music coming through to empower us.

Find Judy's music at
http://cdbaby.com/cd/judybayse.
Contact her at judybayse@sbcglobal.net.

Kathy Byers, Chatham, New Jersey

Coming from a large family, fourth of five children, and being one of forty-one cousins, was cause for celebration quite frequently. Outbursts in song by my mother's five harmonious sisters while she played piano by ear, and by my dad and his brother, Uncle Harry, were the center of each fun (and lengthy, more-like-a-marathon) family gathering.

I started singing at around age three, picked up the guitar at age twelve, leading songs around any campfire I could find. I would go to sleep at night with a Panasonic transistor radio on my pillow (now it's my iPod) and take in all the great folk music of the 1960s while my three brothers blared The Who, Cream and Led Zeppelin in the basement. My dad referred to Led Zeppelin as the "lead balloon."

Being called to encourage and inspire kids of any age today means the most to me in my musical life and career as a children's artist. When young children learn and "echo" back

a song is when I feel most connected, full of purpose, and complete in my mission.

Music does make the world go round, along with, as we all know, passion and love.
Find Kathy's music at
http://www.kathybyers.com and
http://wwwchildrensmusichalloffame.com.

Joanie Calem, Columbus, Ohio

My musical journey began as a child on the long car trips that my family would take, when we would sing endlessly. Somehow, very early, I knew that music was magic. The trips were inevitably full of arguments and irritation, but when we launched into a song, even my teenage siblings begrudgingly sang along. My parents were politically active, and very aware of the power of music to create community, to motivate, to change a mood. I will never forget when my older brother was on his way to an antiwar demonstration in Washington, D.C. (in the 1970s) against the Vietnam War. My father's last words to him before he left were, "If things are getting rough, start singing."

At five, I began badgering my mother to take piano lessons. At seven, after two years of being told that it was too expensive, I bought a piano at an auction with the five dollars of allowance money I had in my pocket. After getting over their shock, my parents realized that I was serious! But the journey I embarked on actually took me away from the sense of musical magic, because my learning experience was one of head-work. I wasn't taught to listen, to improvise, to play what was in my heart, to explore the piano and what it could do; I was taught to read music and reproduce things that others had written.

My first teacher was quite often cruel, chastising me for any mistake, telling me I was stupid. But I still loved music, and my mother thankfully found me another teacher. That experience was actually what propelled me into teaching and performing. I realized that there were those who spread magic with their music, and those who spread shame and unhappiness. I wanted to save other children from being robbed of the beauty of music!

As a musician, a mother, a teacher and a person, I truly believe that music is our deepest language, and innate to everyone. Something in the classical, academic approach has convinced people that you should only sing if you have a "good" voice, that to excel at playing an instrument you must be "talented," and that "good" and "talented" are measurable entities. While I agree that music "learning" comes easier to some children than to others, I do not believe that talent determines ability.

I think love and enthusiasm encourage children into areas that talent alone will not take them. When a child is handed a scarf, a xylophone, a drum, they begin to explore and express themselves. Every child knows how to sing, move, dance and play rhythm instruments. In creating music together, we also learn to listen to each other. I see my role, in the classroom and in performances, as a facilitator, to provide an inviting musical landscape for everyone present to come join our musical community, to listen to and feel the magic!

Joanie currently teaches weekly music classes in local preschools and in daily K–5 music classes at the Columbus Jewish Day School. She teaches piano and guitar privately. She also performs folk music in a variety of local settings, leading programs for groups of all ages. Her goal is to dissolve the sense of performer/ audience, and invite people instead to share a sense of creating community through singing and playing together. Find Joanie's music at http://www.joaniecalem.com. Contact her at jcalem@columbus.rr.com.

Pam Donkin, Millbrae, California

I've been singing all my life. My mother says that as I was being potty-trained, I would sing the commercial jingle, "It's okay to owe Kaye till payday" in perfect pitch!

When I was seven, I had my first stage musical experience as I played Alice in *Alice in Wonderland* at my elementary school. That is where I was bitten by the performing bug. I've been singing and performing ever since!

I was a folk singer in the late 1960s, a jingle singer (coincidentally) in the late 1970s, and when I had children, I sang in their schools, which was the start of my career as a children's music performer and children's music specialist. I have been doing that since the mid-1980s.

I love to sing with and for children. It is not only fun but puts me in touch with my inner child so that I always feel young. What a blessing. I love to be playful with children as we sing, dance or move. Children respond so well to that playfulness. It's as though a door opens and now we have permission to connect with each other through our play and songs.

When I am working with children in music, I am at my happiest and most present. I am very grateful that my work, my play, and my passion have intersected in the wonderful world of children's music. My life's goal is to do what I can to make the world a better place and I love to plant seeds of love and joy through music.

Pam is an award-winning recording artist on

the acclaimed children's record label "A Gentle Wind." She is a veteran teacher and performer and nationally presents family concerts, library performances, assemblies in preschools and elementary schools and workshops for teachers. Find Pam's music at http://www.pamdonkin.com. Contact her at pam@pamdonkin.com or 415-308-4432.

Brigid Finucane, Chicago, Illinois

I come from a family that loves to sing. My mother sang us to sleep every night, and my dad entertained us with corny old songs. The parental gift of a guitar and Joan Baez songbook in eighth grade introduced me to "Childe Ballads" and to a tier of American folksongs I was unfamiliar with. I credit this event with whetting my lifelong interest in music research—where a song comes from (provenance), how it migrated and changed depending on what people/cultures it intersected with. Far into my adult life, I worked as a visual artist and teacher.

This changed in 1993 when my daughter Briana was born. I filled up days and nights with music and songs, and Kindermusik training gave me my first opportunity to start teaching early childhood music while continuing to research cross-cultural music and teaching in Montessori, JCC [Jewish Community Center] and various park-district programs. For me, having a child was a crash course in human development. I found songs that would support my daughter's development and used them with the children in my music classes. I came to see the voice as the original instrument and the heart as the original beat. Watching parents, teachers and children in my classes become confident and creative musical beings gave me an unrivaled happiness and a sense of purpose.

Eventually, I started teaching early childhood music at Merit School of Music in Chicago. I teach on-site family classes and have developed a program that teaches five-to seven-year-olds how to read and write music and play the glockenspiel. In my off-site classes, I teach many non-English-speaking students, and have developed a curriculum where I teach English through music. The reductive nature and power of music to engage makes it the perfect tool to present concepts, explore emotions and promote peaceful community while exposing the children to lyrical and expressive language.

Musical games and dances are important components. The fascinating new research on brain development and music and literacy has made the work even more exciting while feeding my love of research. The more I teach, the more I love it. I learn as much from my students and families as they do from me, and the opportunity to learn and grow is infinite. I've become familiar with people and other cultures that would have remained closed to me. Sharing the joy of singing and music-making with them has proven to be a powerful and profoundly moving way of connecting to them, the past and the future.

Contact Brigid at 1749 W. Granville, Chicago, Illinois, 60660, 773-743-4773. The Merit School of Music is at 38 S. Peoria, Chicago, Ilinois, 312-786-9428.

Fran Friedman, Wayland, Massachusetts

On weekends, my family and I would pile into the car to visit my grandparents. We would immediately break into song, with my father singing harmony. It was fun and totally uninhibited. No one was ever made to feel self-conscious about their voice. We just sang. There in the back seat of our family car was the birth of my pure joy and love for music.

That joy stayed with me my entire life. I remember feeling awestruck when I sang my first harmony in the car. It worked! It was fun! That confidence followed me into middle school, when I taught myself guitar and formed a folk group. That was back in the 1960s, and we sang a lot of politically based music. We were regulars for the school assemblies. While I continued to sing during college in local coffee houses, I decided to take a different path for my career.

I received a Ph.D., and worked for twenty-four years as a clinical audiologist. It was fun, but my love for music and for working with children sent my heart back to music. This time, instead of political music, it was music about caring and loving children and making them feel special. The songs I selected for my CDs take that thread of caring throughout.

I was never a good reader in school, and had to work hard. Learning didn't come easily to me. How I gained the feelings of confidence and competence (the building blocks of self-esteem) to achieve what I did, was through my earlier experiences with music. You never know where music is going to take you, but having it can take you far.

Fran is a children's musician and recording artist and has won a Parents' Choice Gold Award for her children's CDs. Find her music at http://www.franfriedman.com. Contact her at 508-358-1614.

Purly Gates, Driftwood, Texas

Why I do what I do . . .

When I was a little girl, my mom was a "den leader" for my brother's Cub Scout pack. She always took me to the meetings,

and I loved watching her teach arts & crafts projects to the boys. That undoubtedly influenced my life path.

Years later, on my way to high school each day, I passed by the local public library. Once I discovered the "Record Room" at that library, my life was never the same. I listened to music from all over the world as well as traditional American and contemporary folk music.

I also discovered that I learned better through listening than reading, and that there were all kinds of things you could learn about by listening to recordings…including history, foreign languages, social studies, music and of course—many great songs! I learned those songs by playing along with the records, on my guitar.

As a junior in high school, I made another important discovery. My social studies teacher gave the class a homework assignment one day—to write a paper about the subject we were studying. I cringed, as usual, at the thought of having to write a paper. But after class I told the teacher I "knew" a song on the subject. When she asked me if I would be willing to sing the song for the class—*in place of writing the paper*—my life was forever changed.

The power of music and the options it offered were absolutely tantalizing. So I went home and actually finished learning the song, and did indeed sing it for the class. That song was "Deep River Blues" (learned from one of those library records), and I've been singing it ever since!

Much later in my life I taught preschool, then third grade and K–8 music, but went back to working as a musician and a teaching artist. I like this work because it's fun, flexible, educational and involves working with young folks…because I love teaching, and because it feels good to share some of my values through my work.

One day a music partner told me about an assignment for a college class he was taking. I was so intrigued, I asked him for all the details he could remember. I wrote them all down, and soon tried making the homemade instruments my friend had described. That day, my life had taken another turn…and I've been going down that road ever since, leading instrument-making workshops for students, teachers and counselors, too.

What is the impact on young children, and the grow-ups who love them—including family and educators . . .

During my instrument-making workshops I have seen parents sit down to help their children, and get more excited than the kids! Both young folks and grown-ups have been empowered to try other projects once they see how much fun it is to make things with your own hands, rather than buy them. And they also learn that you don't necessarily need to do this with new materials. Recycled materials can be turned into pretty cool instruments!

The emphasis of my concerts is on participation. Being part of a big group of people singing together is a terrific way to experience both community, and the wonderful feeling of being surrounded by "live" sound. I always ask both students and teachers to help out on stage. I see teachers' faces reflecting their pleasure in both the "lighter moment" and the awareness that fun and education can and do go well together.

I sing songs I've written, and songs from other folks. Many of them were learned at CMN gatherings, and they all have a message. The messages, I think, will help build a better world. Since songs have a good "sticky" factor…children do indeed remember them.

I also tell my audiences that I LOVE my job. And it's a strong message: life is full of choices; choose what you really enjoy; follow your heart; your passion and your work can meld together seamlessly. No one is too young or too old to hear that! I really do believe we can change the world, one day and one person at a time.

Purly is a singer/songwriter/multi-instrumentalist who spends her time in both Texas and New England, presenting concerts and workshops at elementary schools, rec centers, camps, festivals, parks, conferences and staff trainings. She sings about literacy, diversity, the environment and more, and has released four recordings for young folks on these subjects. Her song "I Can Read" was commissioned by the Texas State Library as the theme song for its 2004 Summer Reading Club. Find her music at http://www.purlygates.com. Contact her info@purlygates.com or 877-431-7921.

Judy Caplan Ginsburgh, Alexandria, Louisiana

Since 1981, I have made my living as a professional singer specializing in early childhood music. I have always known that music is magical, and it is a personal mission of mine to make sure that everyone experiences this magic. In 2003, I began a nonprofit organization that brings arts experiences into healthcare settings. We use music, art, dance and spoken word to help people relieve stress and pain, express their emotions, relax and ultimately feel a sense of wholeness and healing. I now witness daily the power and the magic of music. We, as professionals in the field, are mere instruments, and it is important that we share our God-given gifts with as many people as we can. We must spread the magic.

For me, music is the best medicine. It is my "drug" of choice. If we can expose people to the joy and expressive nature of music, we can help our society become healthy and whole. When we share music with children, we are leaving a wonderful legacy with our newest generations. A society is always remembered for its culture. So, let's all keep contributing to our future.

Judy is a multi-award-winning singer/songwriter/educator and the founder of Central Louisiana Arts and Healthcare, Inc. Find her work at http://wwwjudymusic.com and http://www.artsandhealthcare.org.

Mr. Billy Grisack, De Pere, Wisconsin

I was very lucky to come from a musical family; looking back it was something that I took for granted. My dad and grandpop played jazz professionally, my mom sang pop standards, my grandmom played and sang country-western and my uncles were totally into traditional folk. We would all get together to sing our favorite songs, dance, jam…just spend time together, I miss that very much.

I followed in my father's footsteps and spent over twenty-five years playing music professionally for a living, but it wasn't until my son took me to kindergarten to be his "show and tell" that I performed to a room full of kindergarteners. The kids and I instantly connected, and I realized that this might be a way to do something positive with my musical background. Since then I have tried to create fun/upbeat songs and shows that have strong educational roots. I think I've made a difference.

Today when I'm not performing my language arts program called "six traits of writing" at a library, school assembly concert or as an artist in residence, I try to spend as much time as possible singing and jamming with my talented wife and children in the family music room. Maybe someday one of my kids will be asked to write a story like this…that would be cool.

Mr. Billy is a singer/songwriter and music-marketing consultant. He has recorded five award-winning CDs and performs at over three hundred schools, libraries and daycares every year.
Find his music at http://www.misterbilly.com.

Sammie Haynes, South Berwick, Maine

I've been singing for as long as I can remember—with Nana on piano, with my mother as she composed funny little tunes about pouring milk or climbing on the stepstool, with friends on the swingset, in high school with a folk group, then as a duo and a solo. I was lucky enough to make a living singing folk music for many years.

As a daycare teacher I was prompted to bring in my guitar and sing with the children, which I loved doing. In 1989 my son was born, and I loved singing to him. Every evening I would put him to bed with a lullaby. As he grew, he began asking for more… and more songs. Finally, sweet lullabies gave way to all kinds of music because I was running out of "children's songs." Of course it didn't matter to him—children love all kinds of music—but as a new mother I wanted to sing about kid-friendly things and so began to write songs on the spot. Occasionally, one would stay with me and I'd try to re-create it the next day. It felt really satisfying writing these tender little songs for my young son.

So I continued. He and his friends provided a lot of great material.

I was surprised at how easy it was to transport myself back in time to when I was a child. I easily recalled some of the wonder, hurt, confusion and naivety that I'd once felt and that my son was experiencing. It helped me find a voice for my writing.

Writing and performing children's music has been truly inspiring and delightful. It took years to figure out what I was supposed to do in my life. Other than being a parent, I can't think of a more satisfying and challenging experience. I feel very committed to working, playing and singing with children. Their future is in our hands.

Sammie is a multi-award-winning children's music writer, performer and recording artist for "A Gentle Wind." She performs in schools, in libraries and at festivals and directs a children's chorus (the Treetops Chorus) and a family chorus in her community. Sammie lives in southern Maine with her husband, the singer/songwriter Cormac McCarthy, and their son, Davis (who will be off to college this year!), their dog, Nikki, and various feathered and amphibious creatures. Find her music at http://www.sammiehaynes.com.

Marie Hopper, Greensboro, North Carolina

Young children are naturally drawn to music-making, especially when it is part of a community activity. Historically, families and friends found many opportunities to gather together to sing and play throughout the course of a year—holidays, courting, barn-raisings, etc….In our culture of individual achievement, passive consumerism of music performed (or not!) by others, and disjointed families, community music-making has fallen woefully to the wayside. Enter

a wide variety of programs designed to bring back a culture of music-making.

Trained as an elementary school music teacher and classical musician, I found myself drawn to the world of early childhood. In my part of the world, the vast majority of children are in a preschool setting all day and all week long.

By bringing music to the children, especially to those children whose parents are unable to find the time to bring them to any enrichment programs outside of the preschool setting, all children are given an opportunity to experience the joy of singing and playing in a musical way as a community.

Over the years, I have consistently found that the children relax and feel freer in their creative expressions as a result of participating in a weekly music class. They learn how to do so much more than make music—they learn how to get along, to share and to enjoy each other's company in a non-competitive, mutually beneficial way. Love really does grow when a group of children make music together!

Marie is the founder and director of Musicare RWITHC, a preschool program. A classically trained clarinetist, Marie has been bringing the joy of music to young children since 1985. Find her music at http://www.musicare-usa.com. Contact her at P.O. Box 5715, Greensboro, North Carolina, 27435, 336-375-3861.

Dave Kinnoin, South Pasedena, California

My good friend Tim Cain said he believes his main job is bringing joy to children, and I agree with him. I must keep the love of music and lyrics alive in everything I do in my career of writing and singing songs for and with kids. I must listen carefully to their stories and honor their thoughts and feelings. I must be patient with those who are reluctant to share, and must never press them beyond a point I must be sensitive enough to figure out.

Not every kid wakes up happy. Some are terribly burdened in ways not easily known. These kids especially need joy. They need moments of freedom when they are just as lucky, just as happy, as other kids. Five minutes of joy in a life too cluttered with emotional pain can be immeasurably valuable. I must be vigilant in remaining a good steward of the trust these young hearts place in me.

Dave. Kinnoin has written and produced hundreds of songs for Disney, the Muppets and dozens of other companies big and small. He is the winner of a Parents' Choice Gold Award and a recording artist for "Song Wizard Records." His work can be seen and heard at http://www.songwizard.com/

Juliette McDonald, Cupertino, California

My childhood:

The best memory my heart held onto from my childhood was singing in my family. We sang songs in church, songs when doing housework, and sang miles of songs while traveling in the car. One of my favorite things to do was sitting outside the house where the bathroom window was cracked open so I could hear my father's warm and comforting voice singing in the shower. My mother had the most beautiful voice, and when they sang together it sent chills down my back. During the holidays, all six of us kids would sing every Christmas song you could think of over and over again, and since I was the fifth child, I learned all the songs my siblings knew before me, and what I learned on my own in school and wherever music was played. I loved singing! With all that would one day pull us all apart, singing was the one thing that brought us all together.

About my history to present:

I tried to turn off my desire to love music. I tried to listen to everyone in my world to do the "right" thing, so I went to business school, learned a trade…but over the years I worked as a melted candle separator, Easter basket stuffer, T-shirt decal ironer, waitress, gardener, computer operator, and finally that brought me back to my real job, preschool teacher/director, where I was right back to singing every day and where my inspiration for writing songs came from.

I spent hours every day singing with the children in my in-home preschool. At circle time I would start a story-song from my head and draw simple pictures on large paper. The songs were funny, simple, easy, and came into my head and out to the world and [were] lost. That is when I started to record them on a cassette player as I told the stories, and later they evolved and found their way into the songs that are now on my three CDs and will be on the new CDs to come.

Why do I do what I do?

Music is the one thing that crosses over all boundaries and offers a space for us all to be as one. It's like laughter and tears and all emotions put to rhythms and melodies that everyone can relate to. It's the one thing that has been consistent in my life. I love to introduce children to their first experience of music, bringing them themes that are inclusive to their understanding. I love to help guide parents on how easy it is to offer music and how important it is to the development of the child. As I facilitate learning, I am also inspired by the children around me.

My imagination is stimulated into writing new children's songs. I have written ballads, pop tunes, educational songs, but my favorite songs are the ones that make you laugh. Someone asked me, "What would you do if you did not do music with children?" I could not answer that question. This is the perfect fit for me, and it's taken me my whole life to come to understand and accept that. I love my work!

Juliette performs and teaches around the United States, especially in California. Find her music at http://www.juliettemcdonald.com and http://www.cdbaby.com.

Kathy Reid-Naiman, Aurora, Ontario

This was not my first choice of careers; I thought that I would be a folksinger…lots of money in that. However, when my first child was two years old, I joined a cooperative nursery school. We all shared the tasks of keeping the school clean, preparing snacks, etc., and I very quickly learned that if I volunteered to bring my guitar in to sing with the children at music time, I would be occupied when the heavy-duty work was being done.

I didn't think that I knew very many kids' songs, but as the weeks went by, more and more songs came drifting back to me. It became an outlet for music in a time that I had very little energy for adult music, and I loved singing with my own children too. It brought back so many memories of how much music meant to me as a child, and how I cherished the teachers who shared music with me along the way.

I think that I can truthfully say that children's music changed my life and continues to enhance it. Now I am a folksinger, and I write a lot of songs and rhymes for children, but my greatest satisfaction comes from singing a brand-new song with a group of parents and children and have them all join in as if they had known it forever.

Kathy has worked as a musician, singer, educator, recording artist, record producer and the president of Canada's foremost early childhood recording company: Merriweather Records Ltd. Find her music at http://www.merriweather.ca. Contact her at Kathy@merriweather.ca or 109 Crawford Rose Dr., Aurora, Ontario, ON LAG 4S1, 905-841-1879.

Terri Roben, Ballston, New York

I love to sing and play music with all ages, but especially children. My earliest memory is of lying on my stomach while my mother bent over the crib, rubbing my back and singing "Go to sleepy little baby, go to sleepy little baby: When you wake, you'll patty patty cake and ride a shining little pony, ride a shining little pony . . ." My daughter, now twenty-three, says her earliest memory is of me singing to her on our front porch and playing guitar. Music is a powerful memory maker!

Find Terri's music at http://www.terriroben.com.

Sally Rogers, Pomfret Center, Connecticut

I sing for children because parents and grandparents have forgotten how. Children now go to bed with a CD (or even a video!) playing in the background as they lull their way into slumber. They watch television and see others sing with enormous bands backing them up. The simplicity of singing games, jump-rope rhymes and nursery rhymes is rapidly disappearing from our culture. Babies rarely bounce to old rhymes on their parents' laps.

If not for music teachers and other children's and family musicians, these traditional musical entertainments could well become extinct in our culture. Traditional songs are the time-tested truths of our musical inheritance and the basis for much of our more "serious" classical music. So I am among the culture bearers who teach children that they can make music wherever they are. Our voices are our best instrument. They are given to us at birth to give voice to our thoughts, joys, loves and fears. We need to remind ourselves that we still have them. And sing!

Sally is a traveling musician. Find her music at http://www.sallyrogers.com. Contact her at sally@sallyrogers.com or P.O. Box 285, Pomfret Center, Connecticut, 06259, 860-974-3089.

Jean Schwartz, Boston, Massachusetts

For many years I ran a drop-in sing-along for preschoolers and their grown-ups one day a week in my home. I charged a modest flat fee per family, so as it happens, I attracted a lot of families with twins! One year a mom came with twin girls who were about three and a half years old. One was developmentally and somewhat physically challenged. While her sister participated in all the hand-clapping and jumping and everything else that went on, she didn't. She'd stand up with the other kids with her mom's help, but then pretty much remain motionless, only rarely moving even her eyes until it was time to sit down again.

One lovely Spring day, after they had been coming to my house for many months, I was singing a dancing and jumping song which we did every week, and the kids were dancing. Then we got to the jumping part, and the little miracle happened. She looked at the other kids jumping up and down and while her feet never left the floor, she started to bend over from her waist—up and down, up and down—and a tiny smile crossed her face. I looked at her mom, and there were tears in both our eyes, but we smiled a knowing smile at each other and kept singing.

Jean has been making music for and with children in preschools and libraries in and around Boston for over fifteen years. Find her music at http://www.jeanschwartz.com.

Maureen Schiffman, Novi, Michigan

When I was a child, my parents filled the house with piano music (my father played and composed and sang), and they both taught ballroom dance in our basement. They played lots of records filled with contemporary music as well as classical. When they were busy, I'd put on the classical and act out scenes, such as being out in a boat in the sea when a storm comes, always with happy endings. I danced around and kept time with the beat. When I was seven, I began jazz, tap and ballet lessons, until I was a graduate in high school.

We were on TV all the time, living in Detroit. I performed at my high school's talent shows. It was wonderful for my self-esteem. I was thin and muscular from all the practicing. When I was ten, I took piano lessons for a few years, but didn't like it. Fortunately for those lessons, I was able to get the basics to musical instruments and taught myself guitar, mandolin, ukulele, dulcimer and played the synthesizer from high school to present.

After becoming a teacher, earning a degree from the University of Michigan, I taught preschool, involving the children in puppetry, song, dance and acting. I taught them positive self-esteem and about their world, through all these gifts I either learned or experimented with. I now write programs for the National Library Summer Reading Themes each year and perform, bring children up on stage to perform and become stars with me. I even have a puppet stage that fits on a wheelchair.

I wrote the song "Sing a Little Happy Song" on a day that I was feeling rather down, and it's the best movement song that I have seen my audiences react to! I always have music playing at home for me, and it ranges from Celtic to African Pigmies singing! I still love to dance, and when my son was born, I exposed him to music as well. He writes his own songs now too.

Maureen is involved in children's entertainment, music, puppets, movement and magic. She's a member of the Detroit Puppeteer's Guild. Find her music at http://www.hometown.aol. com/mesa122/maureenschiffman.html.

Patricia Shih, Huntington, New York

Ever since I was a child, I have always felt that music can be a powerful tool for educating the mind as well as opening the heart. Growing up in the 1960s and 1970s, I learned firsthand how music can inform minds, shape ideas and attitudes, motivate action and inspire movements.

I started my professional career as a musician, singer and songwriter as a child, at the age of fifteen. Even then I was writing the kind of music I was listening to, and that I would hope would make the same kind of impact on my listeners. Ironically, as a child I sang and wrote for adults; now, as an adult, I sing and write for children!

Back when I started performing for kids and families twenty-two years ago, there was very little "music with meaning" for this audience, and I wanted to extend what I was doing for grown-ups into my new work for children. I wanted my new baby to have songs with substance to learn from and enjoy. I would hope that all young minds could have the opportunity to learn about the bigger world around them through song; thus

the title of my first CD and all my live shows: "Big Ideas!"

Since then many wonderful singers and songwriters are also doing this kind of work, and there is a huge wealth of real quality family music in all styles. Lucky are today's children to have this treasure trove—they only need to look for it!

Patricia has won multiple awards as a singer-songwriter, author and recording artist. Her life in the music business has spanned four decades, including hosting a children's TV show for a year in the New York metro region. Many people sing and record her songs throughout the world. Presently, she is a board member of the Children's Music Network. Find her music at http://www.patriciashih.com. Contact her at patricia@patriciashih.com or Shih Enterprises, Inc., P.O. Box 1554, Huntington, New York 11743, 631 549-2332.

San and Laz Slomovits (Gemini), Ann Arbor, Michigan

We were born in Budapest and lived in Israel before coming to the United States at the age of ten. Living in several countries gave us a chance to see and appreciate many different ways of life, as well as exposing us to the music and instruments of various cultures. We grew up hearing a rich variety of music at home. Our father was a wonderful singer, a cantor in synagogues. The music comes from our father, but whatever it takes to get up in front of an audience and put a song across, that comes from our mother's spirit (though she was not a musician). We have been writing songs, recording and performing for children and families throughout the U.S. and Canada since 1973.

Find San and Laz's music at http://www.geminichildrensmusic.com.

Gigi Weisman, Burlington, Vermont

Music builds community. Singing songs, clapping rhythms and rooms filled with laughter allows people of all ages, abilities, genders, socio-economic and ethnic groups to share and delight in the making of music. It has been my hope to make live music accessible to all. Introducing new songs and keeping the old ones alive is a deeply satisfying experience.

I have used music to help build language, speech, communication and social skills while working with children with autism spectrum disorder and other disabilities. A fun song can be a tool which helps children to talk or acts as a reward for completing a task. It can serve as a connection between adult and child and between children themselves. It can make a difficult task seem easier.

Passing on songs which were sung by Danny Kaye, Burl Ives, Ella Jenkins and Pete Seeger and so many others to the next generation has become more important to me since I realized children are more familiar with theme songs to television shows and video games than with traditional children's songs. Children need the stories and lessons from the songs of old and new.

Gigi is an educational consultant who can also be seen performing throughout the Burlington area. She is currently recording a CD with Joni AvRutick called In a Tree. *She has also sung and played violin on the Fletcher Free Library's sing-along CDs* Sweet Potatoes and Home Grown Tomatoes *and* Little Bit Jumbled and Jivey.

MORE RESOURCES: FINALE

Most of the songs, rhymes and musical activities cited throughout can be found in the "Sing with Me" series, available at http://www.little-folks-music.com.

No computer? No problem. Leave me a message and phone number on my voicemail, and I will sing to you on your answering machine: 734-741-1510.

Read More about It

Bailey, B., and S. Sprinkel. *Brain Smart: What You Can Do to Boost Children's Brain Power.* Audiotape. Oviedo, Fla.: Loving Guidance, 1988.

Beaubien, Brigid. "Elizabeth Cady Stanton's Advice to Parents." *Infants and Toddlers* (Spring 2007).

Bredekamp, S., and C. Copple, eds. *Developmentally Appropriate Practice in Early Childhood Programs Serving Children from Birth through Age 8.* Washington, D.C.: National Association for the Education of Young Children, 1997.

Campbell, Don, and Chris Brewer. *Rhythms of Learning.* Tucson: Zephyr Press, 1991.

Crain, William. *Reclaiming Childhood: Letting Children Be Children in Our Achievement Oriented Society.* New York: Times Books, 2003.

Custodero, Lori. "The Musical Lives of Young Children: Inviting, Seeking and Initiating." *Journal of Zero to Three* 23, no. 1 (2002).

Early Childhood News (November–December 2004) (several articles).

Early Literacy: A Lullaby of Sounds and Words. FACT Coalition at Michigan State University.

ECMMA parents' brochure: http://www.ecmma.org.

Elkind, David. *The Power of Play.* Cambridge: Da Capo, 2007.

Fluegelman, Andrew. *The New Games Book.* Garden City, N.Y.: New Games Foundation, 1976.

Fox, Mem. *Radical Reflections.* Orlando: Harcourt Brace & Co, 1993.

"Getting in Tune…On the Move…The Power of Play . . ." Packets of twenty booklets; available in English and Spanish. http://www.zerotothree.org/bookstore.

Greenberg, Day. "NU Study: Musical Training Helps Brain Process Sound." *Daily Northwestern,* March 29, 2007.

Hannaford, C. *The Dominance Factor.* Arlington, Va.: Great Oceans Publishing, 1997.

———. *Smart Moves: Why Learning Is Not All in the Head.* Arlington, Va.: Great Oceans Publishing, 1995.

"Infants: 'World-Class Learners'" (and numerous other articles). Turn-the-Page Press. http://www.turnthepage.com/articles.php.

International Journal of Music Education 23, no. 2 (2005).

Knapp, Mary, and Herbert Knapp. *One Potato, Two Potato: The Folklore of American Children.* New York and London: W. W. Norton and Co., 1976.

Kohn, Alfie. "Five Reasons to Stop Saying 'Good Job.'" http://www.alfiekohn.org/parenting/gj.htm.

Levitin, Daniel J. *This is Your Brain on Music: The Science of a Human Obsession.* New York: Plume, 2006.

Lomax, Alan. *The Folk Songs of North America.* New York: Smithmark, 1960.

Madaule, Paul, *When Listening Comes Alive: A Guide to Effective Learning and Communication.* Norval, Ont.: Moulin Publishing, 1994.

Meyerhoff, Michael K. "The Power of Play: A Discussion about Early Childhood Education." Brochure. Lindenhurst, Ill.: Epicenter Inc.

"Nature." *Young Children* (January 2008).

Neely, Linda Page, Susan Kenney, and Jan Wolf. *Start the Music, Strategies.* Reston, Va.: MENC, 2000. http://www.menc.org/.

"Nursery Rhymes, Songs, Fingerplays." Brochure. West Bloomfield Township Public Library. http://www.wlbib.org.

Orff Echo (Spring 2006) (several articles).

Seeger, Ruth Crawford. *American Folks Songs for Children.* Garden City, N.Y.: Doubleday, 1948.

Spotlight on Early Childhood Music Education. Reston, Va.: National Association for Music Education, 2000.

Tick, Judith. *Ruth Crawford Seeger: A Composer's Search for American Music.* Oxford: Oxford University Press, 2000.

Web Sites

American Montessori Consulting: http://www.amonco.org.

American Orff-Shulwerk Association: http://www.aosa.org/.

Arts from the Inside Out: http://www.sparkplugdance.org/curricula/arts-from-the-inside-out.pdf.

Children's Defense Fund: http://www.childrensdefense.org.

Children's Music Network: http://www.cmnonline.org.

Creative Dance Center: http://www.creativedance.org.

Early Childhood Music and Movement Association: http://www.ecmma.org.

Ecewebguide: http://www.ecewebguide.com/movement.html.

The Gordon Institute for Music Learning: http://www.giml.org.

Grandparents.com: http://www.grandparentsmagazine.com.

Kiddles.com: http://www.kiddles.com.

Music for Young Minds: http://www.musicforyoungminds.com.

Music Moves for Piano: http://www.musicmovesforpiano.com.

National Association for the Education of Young Children: http://www.naeyc.org.

National Association for Music Education: http://www.menc.org/.

National Institute for Literacy: http://www.nifl.gov.

National Institute of Mental Health: http://www.nimh.nih.gov/.

Organization of American Kodaly Educators: http://www.oake.org.

Parenting Press (online newsletter): http://www.parentingpress.com.

Parents' Music Room: http://www.bbc.co.uk/music/parents/yourchild/childdev_chart.shtml.

A Place of Our Own: http://www.Aplaceofourown.org.

Preschoolers and Creative Dance: http://www.sparkplugdance.org/preschool.php.

Zero to Three: http://www.zerotothree.org.

Activity Books

Brashears, Deya, and Sharron Krull. *Circle Time Activities for Young Children.* http://www.playfulconnections.com/about/about.html.

Valerio, Reynolds, Taggart Bolton, and Edwin E. Gordon. *Music Play.* http://www.giamusic.com.

Weissman, Jackie. *Higgelty Piggelty Pop.* http://www.ghbooks.com.

Musicians

Also see chapter 18 for more information on wonderful children's musicians.

Julie Austin: http://www.julieaustin.com.

Laurie Berkner: http://www.Twotomatoes.com.

Bev Bos: http://www.turnthepage.com.

John Feirabend: http://www.giamusic.com.

Cathy Fink and Marcy Marxer: http://www.cathymarcy.com.

Woody Guthrie: http://www.woodyguthrie.org.

Jo Kirk: http://www.wejoysing.com.

Lynn Kleiner: http://www.musicrhapsody.com.

Nice Warm Socks: Wren Singers and Friends: http://www.Nicewarmsocks.org.uk.

Ruth Pelham: http://cdbaby.com/cd/gentlewind10.

Raffi: http://www.Musicoutfitter.com.

Pete Seeger: http://www.peteseeger.net.

Ruth Crawford Seeger: American Folk Songs for Children: Rounder Records: http://www.rounder.com.

Jill Trinka: http://www.johnsmusic.com.

Two of a Kind: http://www.twoofakind.com.

Dan Zanes: http://www.danzanes.com.

Sources for Instruments and Materials

Connie's Educational: http://www.connieseducational.com.

Empire Music: http://www.empire-music.com.

Grover Musical Products: http://www.grotro.com.

Music for Little People: http://www.mflp.com.

Rhythm Band: http://www.rhythmband.com.

Teachers' Discount: http://www.tdbestprice.com.

West Music: http://www.westmusic.com.